AUTUMN
GARDENS

AUTUMN
GARDENS

ETHNE CLARKE
PHOTOGRAPHY BY
JONATHAN BUCKLEY

SOMA

First published 1999 in Great Britain by David & Charles. North American edition published 1999 by Soma Books, by arrangement with David & Charles.

Soma Books is an imprint of Bay Books & Tapes, 555 De Haro St., No. 220, San Francisco, CA 94107.

Designed by Dick Malt

For the Soma edition:
North American editor: Leslie Tilley
Proofreader: Cynthia Nims
Production: Jeff Brandenburg

Library of Congress Cataloging-in-Publication Data on file with the Publisher

ISBN 1-57959-049-7

Printed in Singapore by C.S. Graphics Pte. Ltd.

10 9 8 7 6 5 4 3 2 1

Distributed by Publishers Group West

ACKNOWLEDGMENTS

My sincerest thanks to Anna Mumford and her editorial team, for the support they gave me, Jonathan Buckley and Dick Malt in putting this book together—that we managed to do it across half a continent and the Atlantic Ocean is due in part to the wonders of e-mail, but mostly to Anna's faith in us and her willingness to just let us get on with it. I've worked with many editors, and she is one of the very best. We owe a huge debt of gratitude to the many garden owners who allowed us to include their gardens in this book; without their cooperation it would not have been possible to illustrate the special beauty of autumn.

Many of Jonathan's photographs were taken in gardens that have had an enormous influence on my development as a gardener—none more so than Mark Brown's garden in Normandy, France. He has a very light touch in the garden, and looks unfailingly to the native landscape for his inspiration. He examines each flower in depth to understand its color setting and the shape and texture of each leaf to help him discover its ideal partner. As a result, Mark's gardens, founded in harmony, transmit an almost spiritual tranquillity. Now I too try to look deeper, to understand as well as know my plants.

In Norfolk, England, Alan Gray and Graham Robeson have, from our very first meeting five or so years ago, demonstrated what it means to make a garden. When we first met they had not yet started opening their now quite famous garden, the Old Vicarage, East Ruston, to public view; I recall Alan saying that he wasn't sure anyone would want to see what they were doing! But when a garden is made with such conviction and such commitment to a single vision it stands as a beacon for what the creative process of garden-making is all about. Like all other art forms, it is highly personal, so if you are going to do it, do it for yourself and no one else. Follow your vision.

Having returned to live in the United States, my life has sort of come full circle. However, a new cycle is beginning. I learned my gardening in England, using a palette of plants that, by and large, would struggle to make a decent showing in my almost-tropical new garden. I am on the edge of two climate zones—8 and 9—and surrounded by limestone escarpments; the only way to garden realistically is with na-tive plants or ones from parts of Mexico and Asia that share similar conditions —this I am learning from John Fairey at the Peckerwood Gardens near Houston (where he teeters on the brink of three climate zones!). While it is exciting to begin again at the bottom of the plant-learning curve, I will always value the skills and horticultural knowledge I gleaned from friends' gardens and from the many other beautiful gardens of Britain, too numerous to mention here, that I came to know and respect so highly.

It's been an interesting journey.

Ethne Clarke
Austin, Texas
March 1999

CONTENTS

INTRODUCTION

When I first considered writing a book on this subject, I lived in England and my inspiration came from the autumn character of my garden in rural Norfolk. Now, two years later, it is autumn once again, but I am living in south central Texas and making an urban garden not far from downtown Austin. But there are echoes of my English autumn garden all around: the leaves of chinaberry trees are turning egg yolk yellow, and clustered in the fork of each branching bough are pendulous beads of tawny fruit, an image that brings to mind the rosy pink porcelain berries of the Hubei mountain ash that I grew in my garden at Sycamore Barn. As Christmas approaches, I wonder what I will use for my seasonal decorations in place of holly berries from the old field hedge—probably sprays of yaupon holly or maybe the coral fruit of heavenly bamboo. In England, my most treasured autumn tree was sweetgum, so I am grateful to find that it grows well in Austin. The eulalia grasses and dwarf pampas that are so valuable for adding structure

to English autumn gardens serve the same purpose in sub-tropical Texas. During this season, gardeners everywhere are busily planting out pansies and early spring-flowering bulbs, sowing vegetable seed for early crops, and planning and planting perennial borders, shrubs, and trees.

I can see that there are other similarities, but perhaps the most remarkable one of all is the way the warm days and cool nights in the Texas hill country produce in the landscape the sort of soft hues you find in handwoven tweed, reminding me and expatriate English friends of seasonal foliage in England. It might sound fanciful, but I can almost imagine myself back in Norfolk—were it not for the bright blue skies and temperatures around 85 degrees. In England we cherish the few sweet warm days of Indian summer when the temperature climbs back up before the winter cold sets in; I arrived in Texas in time to experience the pleasurable

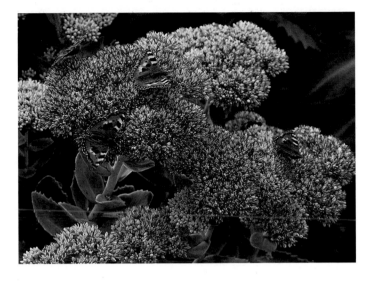

LEFT *Contemplating autumn, many gardeners think first of the brightly colored maples, like* Acer palmatum *'Sango-kaku', the popular cultivar of Japanese maple.*

ABOVE *Butterflies are attracted to autumn-flowering stonecrops.*

PREVIOUS PAGES *The fiery foliage of a vine-covered tunnel in the Edwardian garden at Powis Castle in Wales frames the path.*
INSET *A contrast of shape and textures enhances the reflected glory of majestic pampas grass* (Cortaderia selloana) *and colorful staghorn sumac.*

few cool days that herald the onset of autumn. The climatic symmetry ends there.

Drought is another contributing factor to fine autumn colors—a dry summer season, no matter where you live, will enhance the tints of fading foliage. It will also have an impact on the plants we choose to grow, since gardeners everywhere are becoming more conscientious about the amount of fresh water they are willing to lavish on their gardens. When I gardened in East Anglia, I knew Beth Chatto's dry garden as the English prototype for a new approach to ecologically friendly horticulture. Careful soil preparation meant digging in plenty of rotted manure and compost to supplement the moisture-retentive qualities of the planting beds. This was married to a highly selective choice of plants, focusing on only those that are suited to dry, free-draining conditions. Rereading Beth's book, *The Dry Garden*, along-side Texan horticulturist Scott Ogden's *Gardening Success with Difficult Soils,* I feel confident that the dry-gardening skills I learned in my English garden will be put to good use in Austin; general garden practice does not alter no matter where you live.

DIG THAT GARDEN

Autumn is unquestionably the busiest time of the gardening year. Digging features as the main activity (so it is time to brush up on stretching exercises to prevent strained muscles, and stock up on Epsom salts for soothing baths). New beds and planting areas can be prepared, established perennials dug up and divided as they die back, seed gathered, or root and stem cuttings taken for propagation. Don't be in too much of a hurry to tidy up, or you risk depriving yourself of some of autumn's glory in the faded seedheads and foliage dotting the flower garden. However, do make good time while the sun shines to do the digging.

Tilling the soil is a gardener's most fundamental activity; you can't garden if you don't dig. Some people, including myself, might wish this were otherwise; too much energetic spadework in the early years of gardenmaking has left me with a back and shoulders that squeal in anguish at the onset of autumn—but maybe it's the weather, not the sight of the spade. But, as in many things in life, there are levels of commitment to this activity and there are ways to minimize it.

We dig to loosen the soil, to incorporate nutrients, and to improve drainage, thereby making it easier for the plants we grow to thrive in the artificial environment of the garden.

ABOVE *Autumn is the season of mists and mellow fruitfulness. The soft, moist air and low light at this time of year create special effects in the garden that can be exploited by the observant gardener.*

Autumn is the best time of year to dig, because then the rain, snow, and frosts of winter will further break down the overturned clods of earth, making it easier to create a fine tilth in spring when it is time to plant and sow.

There are different levels of digging: single digging, where you turn over soil only to the depth of one spade blade and confine the disturbance to the top 8 to 10 inches of soil; and double digging, which involves moving soil to a depth of at least two spade blades, so that you will probably be digging into the subsoil.

Double digging is only really necessary if you are preparing a previously uncultivated site, like the garden of a newly built house: It breaks up compacted soil, allows compost to be incorporated at deep root level, helps in the removal of deep-rooting perennial weeds, and greatly improves the drainage of water-retentive areas.

Single digging, however, will do the trick for most gardens where new planting areas are being prepared or old ones revitalized. This type of cultivation involves nothing greater than digging to the depth of one spade blade, incorporating the compost that has been spread evenly and generously over the surface of the area being worked.

Dig only the amount you can comfortably lift on the spade, experimenting until you find the pace that best suits your ability. Using a well-made spade—one that has a good sharp edge and that is rolled or shaped at the top where your foot is placed—will help you push the blade into the soil. With the hand nearest the blade hold the shaft with an overhand grip to balance the push-pull action of digging. Hold the spade upright as the blade bites into the soil, then slide whichever hand is not on the handle down the shaft, bending your knees slightly to take the strain off your lower back, and gently turn the soil over. Work rhythmically and pause frequently to straighten your back.

Above all, take time out of your work to enjoy the glow of the autumn sun as it warms your back and shoulders and enjoy the company of the birds that will be close by, ready to pluck any tasty morsel from the path of your spade.

THE SHAPE
OF AUTUMN

There are many natural phenomena by which we mark the passing of the seasons. One of the most interesting of these occurs on a warm, sunny autumn day when a light breeze stirs the coloring leaves and the temperature drops by evening to a brisk coolness. On days such as these, zillions of baby spiders hatch and are carried away by the breeze, which catches their infant spinner threads and deposits the spiders on branches, lawns, garden furniture, and the wilting forms of late summer perennials. The next day, in the early morning, if you walk out into the dew-covered garden, you will see a spidery shroud mantling everything, as each silken filament edged in moisture catches the light to form a silvery tissue of gossamer thread. Events such as this are the mark of autumn—a season to be cherished both for its moments of unexpected beauty and for the pleasure to be had from the commonplace activities (such as digging the soil) that it demands of the gardener.

Composting perfectionists maintain that the heap should be built in careful layers, and turned regularly so the outer edges exchange places with the inner layers, kept covered, and watered if and when it dries out. I'm sure that such scientifically tended heaps produce Premium Grade compost, but the stuff that came out of the corner of the kitchen garden seemed to do the trick, even if it was not completely decomposed and traces of egg shell and old teabags remained to sully its brown crumbly mass.

One of the most rudimentary methods of composting was practiced in my uncle Joe's vegetable patch in Ireland. Pat, the gardener, simply dug the day's vegetable waste directly into the section of garden that was lying fallow—simply to make it easier for the worms to find, "which is why they bury us so deep, you know." This practice made me aware of the importance of compost, of any kind, as a soil conditioner.

The weather at this time of year is often unpredictable, so you will have to make the most of sunny, clement days. Digging and general autumn chores like leaf raking and mulching can't be done in the rain. Also avoid working on beds and planting areas after heavy rain, since the wet soil will compact under your weight.

Pay attention to your compost heaps. As with shirts, every gardener should have at least three—one in use, one ready, and one brand new. Having said that, I have always managed with two (compost heaps, that is). All the vegetable waste from the kitchen went into one, along with leaves, grass clippings, shredded newspaper, the contents of the vacuum cleaner bag and dust bunnies, twiggy branches, and annual weeds pulled from around the garden—but no perennial weeds to pollute the heap. To this I added the occasional spadeful of soil and compost activator—nitrogen-rich chicken manure from my little community of hens. When one bin was full it would be left to decompose while the next was being filled.

ABOVE *Back lighting emphasizes the sinuous frame of an 'Ever Red' Japanese maple (*Acer palmatum *'Dissectum Atropurpureum').*

RIGHT *The bright autumn color of deciduous trees highlights the strong shapes of evergreens such as Nootka cypress (*Chamaecyparis nootkatensis) *with its weeping habit and the glaucous needles of a Colorado blue spruce.*

PREVIOUS PAGES *Autumn accents the broad-spreading crown of the colorful, spring-flowering cherry, (*Prunus *'Mount Fuji').*
INSET *Dew-laden cobwebs span the branches in autumn gardens.*

Except in areas where winter comes very early, it is generally accepted that autumn is the prime season for planting; the soil is warm from summer, and occasional rain encourages transplanted trees and shrubs to produce new growth, helping them settle easily into their new quarters. Even during winter, when top growth is slowed or killed by cold or frost, roots continue to grow underground. A good insulating blanket of mulch 2 to 3 inches thick, applied in early autumn, will aid in the process.

TREES

Trees are the foundation of the landscape; without their presence the garden picture would sprawl before us. Trees anchor their companions to the site. In spring and summer, deciduous and evergreen trees create a background for flower borders and colorful shrubs. If we are aware of trees at all it is for the shadows they cast. In autumn, however, trees arrest our vision. The often startling color of deciduous foliage is followed by the drama of twisted branches and gnarled trunks. Evergreen trees, too, are more prominent in the landscape; their dark mass and solid shapes are thrown into stark contrast with the nakedness of their garden companions.

In 1930, the American landscape architect, Jens Jensen, stated that the building blocks of a garden were "the contours of the earth, the vegetation that covers it, the changing season, the rays of the setting sun, and the afterglow, and the light of the moon," and he admonished all gardeners to work with the natural landscape, using its characteristics as a guide to plant choices and composition. This principle is one sure way of successfully sorting through the myriad beautifully leaved trees until you find the one that must be included in your autumn garden scheme.

Study the native trees in the landscape around you and select the genus with the most autumnal appeal. Expand on the native plant theme by researching species or cultivars within the same genus; you may find alternatives that have showier foliage or bark and would still suit your garden's habitat. Consider, too, why you find the tree appealing. Is it just leaf color that holds your attention, or will the shape and texture of the foliage add to the garden picture during the rest of the year?

The highly individual character of some bark can be made more of by heeding Jensen's words on light. Exploit the light in your garden—sunlight and moonlight—by placing a specimen tree or trees where the foliage will be illuminated or the bark highlighted by the special quality of autumn light in your garden. All gardeners know that they should familiarize themselves with patterns of sun and shade in their gardens so that they know the different planting areas. But aside from this practical aspect of light and shadow is the aesthetic quality of natural light— how the glow of the rising sun slowly warms the eastern aspect of the garden and how the low angle of the setting sun sends rivers of shadow flowing across a lawn. (Depending upon the atmosphere of the garden, light can give a peach or violet tint to the scene, but this is a transient effect and not one that can play too big a part in garden planting plans.)

Most trees respond well to autumn planting, although there are exceptions, among them fleshy rooted subjects such as tulip trees (*Liriodendron tulipifera*) and magnolias. Some evergreens also need protection if planted in the autumn; in any case most should be planted in the early part of the season. But most of the favorite trees for autumn color, such as maple, dogwoods, oaks, and cherry, will do well planted in the autumn, since all these trees begin to go dormant as soon as the soil starts to cool. Their energy is conserved in the roots during this time and is not being utilized to provide top growth.

Trees are available from nurseries as either "bare-root" (not exactly an accurate description since the root ball will be wrapped in burlap), or "container-grown." Large specimen trees are generally lifted mechanically from tree nurseries once all their leaves have dropped; container-grown plants tend to be smaller, with anything from juvenile saplings to more mature trees with trunk diameters up to 2 to 3 inches. Unless you need an instant effect, it is usually not worth the extra expense of purchasing large trees, which really are best dealt with by professional arborists anyway. It seems to take five years for a tree to settle into its new home—no matter what its size when transplanted—and once it has got its toes into the soil, a sapling will grow more rapidly than a more mature tree and will catch up by its eighth or ninth year. The only requirement is patience on the part of the gardener.

Just like general digging in the garden, digging planting holes for trees requires some small degree of method. Have ready a sharp spade and fork, a stake at least 3 to 4 feet long, tree ties, and sharp pruning shears. The planting hole must be at least 1 to 2 feet bigger in diameter than the tree's root ball or container size. Slope the sides of the planting hole rather than making them straight up and down, and make the hole irregular in shape, rather than a perfect circle, to encourage the new root system to spread. The hole should only be as deep as the tree planted at the nursery ground or in the container. You can tell by looking at the trunk—the nursery line is the place where the dark, below-soil section of the trunk meets the light, above-soil section. Plant a little high to allow for settling.

Use the fork to loosen the base and aerate the sides of the hole. Fill it with water, and while it is being absorbed turn your attention to the tree. Always carry the tree by the pot or transport it in a wheelbarrow; don't lug it around by the trunk as the weight of the soil-laden root ball puts enormous strain on the roots. Remove the container or wrapping and inspect the roots. Cut away any that are damaged or withered roots but no others. If the roots are matted or have circled the inside of the container, tease them out with your fingers.

Place the tree in the hole, positioning it so its best aspect can be viewed from one particular vantage point, if that is how it fits into your plan, and generally taking care that it is upright and not leaning to one side. Also be sure that you are satisfied with the place you have assigned it in the garden.

It is easier to move perennials and shrubs that prove after time to be in the wrong place than it is to move a tree, so try to get it right the first time.

Backfill with a few shovelfuls of soil to hold the tree steady while you put in the stake. Large specimen trees require backhoes, guy ropes, and hawsers to plant and stake, which is why I said earlier that their handling is best left to professional arborists. But for the average nursery-stock tree in a 1 gallon container, an oak tree stake is sufficient. Place it on the side of the tree that faces the prevailing wind and about 2 inches from the base of the tree; then pound it into the base of the planting hole until it feels securely embedded. The stake does not need to extend higher than 12 to 18 inches above ground. Although some gardeners advocate stakes tall enough to reach the lowest branch of the young tree—up to 2 to 3 feet—a short stake allows the tree to sway and move in the wind, and this movement encourages a stronger root system to develop more quickly, anchoring the tree in its new home. Then put the tree tie in place; most come with a spacer collar so that the tie can be attached, in a figure eight and the tree is held securely but not strangled. Old nylons, strips of plastic bag, or rope *will not* do. They are not only ugly, but they can harbor pests and damage the bark by constant abrasion. Nor will they allow for growth as the tree trunk gets bigger.

Backfill the planting hole, breaking up the clods of earth as you go. When the hole is full, use your foot to tamp down the soil gently around the base of the tree and to firm the soil around the roots. It is not necessary to add any compost,

ABOVE *The view across the terraces at Dinmore Manor, Herefordshire, England, is transformed by the bold autumn colorings of plants such as the Japanese maples and Virginia creeper that dominate the scene.*

CENTER *Even the veil of autumn mist cannot hold back the color of a Japanese maple. These trees take on every shade of red, orange, and yellow to dark purple and are essential to the autumn garden.*

RIGHT *Two types of* Enkianthus, E. campanulatus *in the foreground and* E. cernuus f. rubens *in the background, demonstrate the variation in autumn color to be found among plants in the same genus.*

manure, or fertilizer to the soil when planting trees. The goal is to have the tree establish itself quickly by sending out feeder roots, and if the food is within easy reach, the roots will not fan out into the surrounding soil.

After planting the tree, water it well to settle it into the soil. If the season is dry, water at least once a week right up until the first freeze. Use leftover loose soil to build a berm around the planting hole. This creates a small well that can be filled with water, which will then trickle down to the roots rather than run off into the surrounding area. Finally, lay down a good blanket of mulch around the foot of the tree, but keep it out of direct contact with the trunk.

The only pruning that should be done at this stage is removing weak, twiggy growth along the main trunk and cutting out any damaged branches. Any crossing branches can also be removed: Cut away the one that contributes least to the overall shape of the crown, and if there is a double leader (the main upward growing shoot), prune away the weakest of the two.

Most deciduous trees can withstand winter conditions, but evergreen trees planted in autumn may need to be screened with horticultural fabric to protect the foliage from winter winds. Spray-on antidesiccants can minimize moisture loss by giving foliage a protective coating but they must be reapplied weekly to be effective.

SHRUBS

As I wrote in my book *Leaf, Bark and Berry*, the landscape appears in layers, and beneath the canopy of trees is the understory, occupied by shrubs, perennials, annuals and biennials (the ephemeral layer), and groundcover.

Shrubs are the walls of the garden, filling the space beneath trees and shaping our view of the landscape. The windows created by ornamental foliage direct our vision outward or draw the surrounding landscape into the garden. As hedges, shrubs screen the distant view to create an inward-looking realm.

Evergreen shrubs are most often used as hedges, since their foliage is permanent. The shade they cast also becomes a permanent feature of the garden, and it is difficult to grow anything below their dark mass. Deciduous shrubs, on the other hand, admit the warmth and moisture that the perennial and ephemeral layer requires during the growing season. Groupings of deciduous shrubs selected for their mutual growing requirements of sun or shade, acid or alkaline soil, and moist or dry ground can make a significant addition to the garden all year round. Many have highly decorative flowers, delicious perfumes, elegant habits of growth, showy bark, or brilliant color.

One of my favorite shrubs, which lacks only fragrance, is *Viburnum plicatum* 'Mariesii'. It holds its branches in graceful spreading tiers, and in summer they are covered along their uppermost edges with pale white flowers that look like tiny saucers balancing on a table edge. The long oval leaves droop down either side of the branch, and in autumn they turn a rich burgundy-red before dropping to reveal the spreading structure. As is often the case, another species within the genus offers possibly even greater charms. *V. bodnantense* 'Dawn' is upright growing and has richly scented flower clusters in early spring and glowing vinous tones in autumn. Cutting branches of this shrub during late winter and early spring both provides indoor decoration and ensures that there will be plenty of new growth to produce flowers the following year.

Planting a shrub is much the same as planting a tree, except that the shrub will not require any staking. Unlike trees, which can stand as solitary specimens in a garden scheme, shrubs look best in groups. This was recognized by William Robinson, who was one of the earliest English garden writers to advocate the use of mixed perennial and shrub borders to create natural habitats for less common and "difficult" flowering plants. Robinson exercised his theories at his home, Gravetye Manor, in Sussex. He wrote of his experience in several books, most notably *The English Flower Garden* and a journal on the development of Gravetye. Of shrub planting, he wrote that he liked to plant "in bold beds to screen rather steep and awkward banks, and at the same time to give a home to many fine things that would not be very well placed in the flower garden." He advised that the edge of a shrub planting should be undulating and irregular and that tall-growing flowers and bulbs such as lilies should be worked in along the outer edges to give a soft and pleasing line.

Mixed shrub borders are not maintenance free. Left untended, shrubs have a way of growing together into a large homogeneous mass. They must be pruned carefully to thin out and, to some degree, sculpt the shrubby mass into pleasing forms so that each plant clearly retains its identity.

CLIMBERS

One of the plants that most readily leaps to mind when thinking of autumn color is Virginia creeper *(Parthenocissus quinquefolia)*. The archetypal memory many of us share of this plant is of vivid crimson leaves cloaking the brick of hallowed halls, like those of Harvard and Yale and the other "Ivy" League universities of New England—which is regarded as the epicenter of Fall Color. Its relative, silvervein creeper *(P. henryana)* is more subtle in its autumn finery but just as decorative. The silvery white veins on the leaflets become more pronounced as the foliage darkens to ruby red. These plants have in common with English ivy *(Hedera helix)* that they climb by means of adhesive tendrils. Each little filament ends in a sucker that clings to the support. Early on they need some guidance to start the upward climb, but once settled in they will begin their attachment to the support. (It is often advised not to grow ivy against brick or stone walls, because the suckers are thought to erode the mortar. However, some pundits disagree, thinking the ivy offers a protective cloak.

RIGHT *Optimize the autumn light in your garden by arranging plants so that their foliage will be illuminated. Here the familiar shape of the purple-leaved wine grape, (*Vitis vinifera *'Purpurea'), is accented by the glow of autumn afternoon sun, and the red foliage of orach* (Atriplex hortensis var. rubra) *plays off the purple coloring.*

LEFT *The sight of this naturalized patch of the Japanese anemone would warm the heart of William Robinson, whose book* The Wild Garden *promoted planting herbaceous perennials at the woodland edge to give a more relaxed and natural atmosphere to the garden. He also compiled* The English Flower Garden, *in which he described this Japanese anemone as a beautiful plant:* "All good forms of the plant should be cultivated where cut flowers are required in autumn. By having some on a north border, and some on a warm one, the bloom may be prolonged. [They are also] useful for groups, fringes of shrubbery in rich soil, and here and there in half-shady places by wood walks."

ABOVE *A woodland path, winding along the edge of a small lake at the Dingle, in Wales, is framed with gray-barked eucalyptus and a wide variety of multicolored shrubs and small trees.*

RIGHT *Elsewhere in the same garden, mop-headed hydrangeas toss their wine-stained bracts into the background foliage of the serviceberry.*

The jury remains out on this question. English ivy is most often accused of destructive tendencies.)

Members of the grapevine genus, *Vitis*, also give rich autumn coloring, and few climbers are more vibrant than crimson gloryvine *(Vitis coignetiae)*. It has enormous heart-shaped leaves that turn shades of orange, red, and yellow as autumn advances. It is a rampant climber and, like ivy, will quickly cover a supporting wall—and then go on to consume the building. Grapevines climb by way of curly tendrils that emerge at the leaf axil, snaking out in arcs until they find something to wrap around. If you study the direction of the curl, you can sometimes assist this process by wrapping the tendrils around the support in the correct direction.

Five leaf akebia is much loved by Japanese gardeners for the delicacy of its evergreen foliage. It is a dainty plant with tiny leaflets and lanternlike flowers. A twining climber, it wraps around the support in a tangle of sinuous stems.

Climbing roses are the best examples of climbers that use their thorns like grappling hooks to gain a purchase on the support. Other woody-stemmed climbers such as blackberries also rely on thorns, since their stems are not designed to twine. The long canes of this type of plant generally need to be trained and should be pruned and tied into the support in an organized way. However, some roses, like 'Rambling Rector', can be left to their own devices to scramble through trees, spreading their flowers in spring or summer and clusters of dusky hips in autumn through the tree crown.

In small gardens where shrubs as understory filler would take up too much space, climbers can take their place, providing a foliage background for flower borders or a screen to direct or frame the view. If a permanent wall of foliage is required, select one of the evergreen climbers such as *Euonymus fortunei*, perhaps 'Variegatus' with white and yellow striations on the leathery leaves, or a berried evergreen such as one of the pyracanthas.

If year-round cover is not an issue, then your selection is wide; many deciduous climbers will provide colorful autumn backgrounds. Two things to bear in mind when making a choice is how much space you are going to allow the plant and how much time you want to spend keeping it under control. Unlike a tree or shrub, which is geared to making solid, supportive woody growth, most climbers use

their energy to climb, which is why their growth remains supple. As a result, they tend to be quite vigorous. As soon as new growth begins in early spring it is time to begin training and thinning—while the wood is still supple and before the climbing gets out of control.

Climbers can also be trained horizontally, to form ground-cover, although they will always tend to begin climbing any vertical object they bump into. However, a small-leaved grapevine like 'Brant' or an annual ornamental bean like hyacinth bean would be manageable in this situation.

The type of support you select is to some extent determined by the climber's method of climbing. One of the neatest, most efficient supports is made of aluminum wire stretched between vine eyes to form a square grid; the minimum distance between the wires, vertically and horizontally, is 4 inches, and the vine eyes should be long enough to leave at least a 4-inch gap between the wall and the wire. Climbing

plants with tendrils will do well on a wire trellis, and wire has the advantage of being more permanent than a wood trellis. Wood will eventually rot unless it is treated regularly, which means removing the climber. Roses that are trained annually and climbers that are heavily pruned after flowering can be trained against a wood grid, since the pruning provides an opportunity for maintenance.

When planting a climber, always position it at least 12 to 18 inches away from the support, and tilt the root ball in the planting hole so that the top growth is angled toward the support. It is especially important to observe this rule of distance when the climber is grown against a wall. The soil near the foot of a wall will be much drier and less fertile because foundation materials leach out water and can release undesirable minerals or chemicals. When a tree is to be the support, digging the planting hole a foot or more from the base of the trunk will be less likely to interfere with the tree's root system. (Note that in this circumstance the climber will be competing with the tree for nourishment, so give the climber a regular foliar feed during the growing season to provide an extra boost. Once it is established it should be able to fend for itself.)

Make the planting hole large enough to accommodate the root ball and, since most climbers are greedy feeders, add a handful of bonemeal or slow-release all-purpose fertilizer

LEFT *Autumn-coloring vines include the widely known and grown Virginia creeper and Boston ivy. Both vines color ruby red in autumn, and make a splendid contrast to evergreen English ivy.*

to the backfill. If the roots are compacted in the container, separate them gently with your fingers or a hand fork. Spread the roots evenly in the hole, and then add enough soil to hold the plant in position while you guide it against the support. Secure it with a loose tie. Then finish filling the hole, tamping the soil around the plant with your foot. Water the plant regularly until it is established, and keep it mulched to conserve moisture in the soil.

PERENNIALS FOR GROUNDCOVER

There are many prostrate and carpeting perennial plants that will provide excellent groundcover throughout the growing season and well into autumn. Some offer colored foliage year round and thus provide useful contrast beneath shrubs and perennials during summer. Then they blend in with the color of their neighbors as the season changes to autumn.

Harmonious autumn schemes based on yellow could be devised using groundcovers like golden oregano, bright yellow lemon balm, or yellow-variegated periwinkles beneath golden-twig dogwood (*Cornus sericea* 'Flaviramea') and monarch birch *(Betula maximowicziana)* in its autumn color. The full show would last only as long as the birch holds its leaves, but the dogwood and periwinkle can go on well into winter.

In her book, *Groundcover Plants*, Margery Fish described how silver foliage complements red- and bronze-leaved plants like the purple form of smoke tree, (*Cotinus coggygria* 'Purpureus'). Conversely, purple carpet bugle (*Ajuga reptans* 'Atropurpurea') would make a splendid wine-red carpet beneath a silver-leaved artemisia like *Artemisia* 'Powis Castle'. Artemisias have some of the best silver foliage going; Silver King *(A. ludoviciana)* is nearly white and spreads by underground stems. So does Roman wormwood *(A. pontica)*, but give this one a wide berth unless you have plenty of space, as in good soil it quickly forms an impenetrable mat of stems. It has a dull pewter color and frothy texture. Margery Fish describes seeing it carpet the ground beneath apple trees in an orchard.

Before planting an area with groundcover, be sure it is clear of perennial weeds; competition for moisture and nutrients must be kept to a minimum and unsightly weeds would spoil the cohesiveness of the groundcover carpet. The spacing used between plants depends upon the size and vigor of the groundcover. In general, the smaller the plant the closer the spacing, so a dwarf carpeting thyme would be spaced 4 to 6 inches apart (at the center), while larger, more rampant plants like dead nettle could be further apart, say 10 to 12 inches. Plant in an irregular pattern, rather than straight lines, unless you want a formal rhythm to the scheme.

Groundcover beneath deciduous shrubs and trees should be swept to remove fallen leaves, since collected debris encourages disease and causes the groundcover to die off unattractively. Trailing groundcovers like periwinkle can be sheared back to keep their growth in check, and dwarf herbs such as thyme can be gone over with a string trimmer or shears to keep growth tight and to remove flowerheads in late summer.

LAWNS

Probably the most universally popular ground covering plant is grass. More hours are spent tending lawns than any other part of the garden in the quest for perfection, and most of those hours are spent during autumn. There is no question that an even green carpet is the perfect setting for colorful and varied plantings at any time of year.

As with all things, perfection begins with thorough preparation. New lawns grown from seed establish best in the cool days and nights of autumn, when rainfall is more frequent, helping to make germination more even. Try to sow the seed at least six to eight weeks before the first frosts in your area. The type of seed mix you choose will depend upon the climate in your area, the amount of wear and tear the lawn will get, and the appearance you want to achieve.

Lawns do best on level ground in full sun, so beneath trees and on sloping ground use a shade-loving evergreen groundcover instead of grass. Begin by clearing the site, removing all perennial weeds and scraping off annual weeds with a sharp spade. If the area to be sown is thick with weeds, use a herbicide during the summer, when the weeds are growing strongly. It may take several applications to achieve total annihilation, but there's no need to remove the dead weeds, since they can be incorporated into the soil.

To prepare the soil, first dig to at least a spade's depth. Then rake or use a rotary cultivator to break up clods and create a fine texture, adding well-rotted manure or compost as you go. Grass does best in nearly neutral soil, so test the pH—if it is low (acid) add lime to the soil; if it's high (alkaline), dust the ground with sulfur. Firm the seedbed by walking on it or by using a lawn roller. Aim for as level a surface as possible, and take care not to over-compact the soil.

If possible, leave the soil to settle for a week or two (allowing any errant weeds to appear) before sowing the seed. If the soil has dried out more than 1 inch deep, water the ground first. Then use a lawn spreader to sow the seed or scatter it by hand in slow even arcs. Work first in one direction (say lengthwise) using half the seed, and then go back over the ground at right angles to your first pass until all the seed is gone. If you are methodical you will achieve even coverage. Press the seed in by walking across the newly sown area diagonally to lines of seed. Water lightly and regularly until the seed germinates. Use a fine misting spray on a hose attachment rather than a sprinkler because the regular mechanical pattern will wash the seed out of the soil. Set out a scarecrow or else stretch bird netting across the newly sown lawn to protect it from birds, and cordon it off to keep foot traffic off it until the first mowing. Mow the young grass when it is about 3 inches tall. Set the mower blades high for the first clip, and be sure they are freshly sharpened. Subsequent mowings should be close to encourage the grass to thicken up.

Autumn is also the best time to establish new lawns and repair old ones using sod. If an entirely new lawn is not required, but the existing lawn is looking ragged, use sod to replace the unsightly parts. To repair a small area, just remove the existing turf, gently break up the surface of the soil with a sharp fork and lay the sod in place, butting the edges tightly. Trim to fit with a sharp knife and water thoroughly.

Creating a lawn from sod is not complicated. Prepare the planting site just as if you were seeding a new lawn, and do it before the sod is delivered. The idea is to get the lawn laid quickly; the longer the sod is stored, the more it will dry out and turn yellow from lack of light. You will need a plank to walk on as you work and a string stretched tautly across the area as a guide. Lay the first line of sod, sprinkling compost along the seams so that they will knit together as the grass grows. Move the plank onto this line of turf, then lay the next row so that the seams of the second row alternate with the seams of the first row, like bricks work. The key to success is watering—so don't let the sod dry out. In the cool autumn weather the individual pieces will soon grow together to form a healthy green carpet.

PRAIRIES AND SUMMER MEADOWS

In their quest for the natural, many gardeners are rethinking the lawn as a design component, seeking to better complement the more relaxed style of naturalized perennial plantings. In the United States, prairie lawns are increasing in popularity, while in the United Kingdom, meadow lawns are featuring in contemporary schemes.

Some gardeners also feel that a lawn lacks the romance of the prairie. A recitation of the names of the many native species of grass and flowering perennial that populate a true prairie lawn becomes a seductive mantra. Big bluestem and little bluestem, indiangrass, rosinweed, sweet black-eyed Susan, rattlesnake master, compassplant, and prairie blazingstar are

a few of the many species that once carpeted the midwestern plains of the United States, but soon vanished beneath the sodbuster's plow during the great expansions of the nineteenth century. English meadows, once rich with oxlips, primroses, snakeshead fritillaries, lady's slipper orchids, cuckoo flowers, purple self-heal, and other flowering herbs, have all but disappeared beneath the mechanized farming methods of the industrial age.

The swing toward "wild gardening" follows on the heels of increasing ecological awareness wherever people garden. However, not everyone is prepared to convert wholeheartedly to this aesthetic; tradition dies hard, and well-manicured gardens and lawns have long been most people's ideal—even when they come with a high-maintenance price-tag. That is not to say the prairies and meadows don't need care, but the mowing involved happens once or twice a year, rather than every week.

Most beneficially, prairies do not require the use of herbicides, and the flowery carpet becomes a refuge for wildlife.

LEFT *Throughout the year, contrasts of shape are as important as contrasts of color to heighten visual effect, and some perennials offer foliage that is consistently interesting—like this lungwort. Its silver markings are accented by the white blooms of the autumn-flowering* Clematis × jouiniana *'Praecox'.*

RIGHT *Similarly, bright green honey spurge* (Euphorbia mellifera) *seen against a backdrop of the vine* Vitis *'Brant' will be attractive all year round.*

Birds and insects find the seeds and nectar they need to survive, and the benefits to local ecology will be seen in a greatly expanded biodiversity.

Prairie and meadow patches can be a part of a conventional garden design—no need to sweep away the perennial borders and roses—by setting aside a piece of ground. You might select a circular bed set in the center of a sun-filled yard and framed by a gravel path or choose a ribbon of ground along a driveway. By late summer or early autumn, the flowering plants are in their prime and the grasses begin to show ripening seedheads.

In addition to starting with a clear site, a prairie lawn needs a little advance planning. Six weeks before sowing (which happens in early summer) the seed, mixed with sand, must be stored in the refrigerator. This step is essential to the

LEFT *When selecting shrubs and perennials that will share a mixed border, give a thought to the effect they will have on each other throughout the year—not just in summer. In the border at Abbey Dore, in Herefordshire, England, the pampas grass* Cortaderia fulvida *has been placed within arm's reach of* Rosa glauca. *The arch of the rose branches is echoed by the graceful curve of the feathery fronds, and the cherry-red hips of the rose seem to be strung like Christmas lights among the faded grass flowers. In summer, the pale roses and soft glaucous foliage would create just as pleasing a seasonal picture.*

successful germination of most prairie plants. Then, for the first three weeks after sowing, the area must be regularly watered, just like a newly sown lawn. It should also be mulched with clean straw if possible. It is possible to begin a prairie with small transplants or plugs of rooted perennials, but for large areas seed is more economical.

There can be as many as three hundred species of flowering perennials, annuals, bulbs, and grasses in a native prairie—enough to satisfy even the most ardent gardener. (A quick inventory of the perennials growing in my English garden revealed a huge number of prairie plants that were introduced to Britain by plant hunters from the earliest days of colonialism.) Given this diversity, it is probably wise to establish some kind of order when planting, using height, for example. Sow seeds for tall plants like prairie docks and compassplant along the perimeters and keep shorter plants like black-eyed Susan and blazingstar to the front. Eventually, however, the plants will move to where they feel happiest as the prairie habitat shapes itself.

Probably the one fact most people know about prairie gardening is that burning is part of the management routine. And the possibility of burning down the house while gardening has put some people off. Selecting days when the wind is light and blowing in the right direction, as well as setting the fire in a circle so that it burns in on itself and is naturally extinguished, goes a long way toward avoiding a general conflagration. Closely mown grass paths around and through the garden also act as natural firebreaks. Burning every two to fives years, in the early spring, helps the prairie to regenerate by exposing the soil so that it warms earlier, thus assisting the seed of heat-loving prairie plants to germinate more readily. If burning is not an option, mowing in late autumn after seed has been shed will serve the same purpose, as long as the debris is raked off to allow the sun to warm the soil.

Unlike a prairie, meadows are best begun in autumn. Meadows can be established from scratch by sowing a grass and flower seed mix onto prepared soil. Alternatively, a lawn can be adapted by planting flower plugs directly into the turf. I did this successfully in an orchard, using oriental poppies, daylilies, columbines, and cranesbill geraniums. By early autumn, the perennial flowers were fading but the tall grass was turning to seed, and the effect was quite magical in the low evening light.

The preparation for a meadow is the same as for a lawn, except that you must not add fertilizers as you do not want to encourage the grass at the expense of the less robust meadow flowers. By midspring, the grass should be long enough for a first mowing, which will allow light to reach the flowering plants. Perennial plants and bulbs can be naturalized into grass during autumn, so this is the time to experiment with plugging a few species into an area of lawn.

LEFT *The ruby-red autumn colors of Japanese maple are enhanced by an underplanting of the ground-covering evergreen perennial* Ophiopogon planiscapus *'Nigrescens'. The drooping habit of the narrow, dentate maple leaves is echoed by the downward curve of the perennial's simpler leaves.*

LEFT *The thistlelike seedheads of sea holly are set against a cluster of autumn colors, from the straplike red-tinted leaves of New Zealand flax (*Phormium *'Pink Panther'); from* Lapeirousia laxa, *a member of the iris family with bright green, grasslike foliage, topped by sprays of coral-red flowers that turn to beadlike seed pods in the autumn; and the blue-gray* Hebe glaucophylla. *It is rare for plants not to harmonize visually if they enjoy the same growing conditions. All these plants enjoy dry sunny conditions on free-draining soil and would be a good starting point from which to develop a rock or gravel garden bed.*

Autumn is when established meadows are mown; you may find that you will have to scythe down the tall grass or use a string trimmer. As with a prairie, it is important to rake up the debris. This is heavy work, no question about it, but the reward is a wonderful flower-filled tapestry, alive with birds and insects. And you know as well that you have made a contribution, however small, to the continuity of our planet's fragile ecosystems.

INSECT FRIENDS

A grass lawn is a monoculture, and although it may be framed by flower borders, decorated with flowering shrubs, and shaded by trees, it contributes little to the ecology of the garden. Many of the insects that will be attracted to the prairie or meadow plants in a natural groundcovering will be beneficial, devouring aphids, mites, beetles, of all sorts, and so on. And if these insects are not already present in your garden, you can buy them from specialized mail-order firms.

There are two sorts of garden-friendly insect: predators, which devour pests, and parasitoids, which are species-

LEFT *The tall, clump-forming pampas grass,* Cortaderia selloana, *has to be used with care. Place it where the light will catch its feathery plumes.*

RIGHT *Zebra grass (*Miscanthus sinensis 'Zebrinus'*) makes a good focal contrast against the less strident tones of needlegrass (*Stipa gigantea*), glaucous-leaved plume poppy (*Macleaya cordata*) and the foamy seedheads of fireweed (*Epilobium angustifolium*).*

specific. A female parasitoid lays one or more eggs on the host, and the host is eventually consumed by the larvae hatching on or inside the host's body. The mature parasitoid then goes on to find its food in plant nectar or pollen. Lacewings, tiny, delicate emerald-green flies, are the most omnivorous of the predators, followed by ladybugs, the tiny round beetles universally beloved for their endearing black-spotted, shiny red carapace. Both these predators will decimate populations of aphids, spider mites, and scale insects. Parasitoids include a number of different wasps, like the trichogramma, which feeds off a wide range of insect eggs— including butterfly. If you are planting a butterfly garden, avoid *trichogramma*.

Members of the Compositae family are among the favorites of predaceous insects; for example, daisies, goldenrod, yarrow, and members of the sunflower genus *Helianthus*. The central boss of short stamens makes a good "table" for the insects to feed from. Many umbellifer herbs like fennel, myrrh, and dill are also tasty meals for some beneficial insects. Pollen- and nectar-gathering insects enjoy tubular flowers, so sages, catmint, lavenders and thymes should be grown to encourage them. Cover crops (discussed in chapter 3, Harvesting the Garden) will provide a rich assortment of food for these friendly bugs, in addition to fertilizing the soil when it is turned during the autumn dig. In the autumn, beneficial insects need somewhere to shelter, and garden borders where the perennials are left for the interest their seedheads and faded foliage provide will also offer your resident bug population some protection from inclement weather.

It almost goes without saying that it is inadvisable to rely too heavily on pesticides, especially if you want to encourage beneficial insects in your garden. Curiously, it appears that the predators and parasitoids are more susceptible to poison than the unwelcome insects they feed on, so it would defeat the whole exercise to spray the garden with chemicals. If you must resort to sprays, try to use ones that are specific to the pest you are trying to destroy. It is even better to make regular patrols, removing any stems or foliage that are heavily infested. (And what kind of gardener would you be if you weren't on the lookout for trouble.)

BUTTERFLIES

Butterflies are especially welcomed by many gardeners. I'm thrilled at the sight of the monarch butterfly migration that streams through my part of Texas each autumn and will be planting plenty of flowers to welcome them in future years.

Butterflies go through four stages in their life cycle: egg, larva, pupa, and adult, which is the point in their lives when they make their showy debut in our gardens. But it is a brief appearance, and the adult's life span can be as little as two weeks. During that time they must find a mate, lay the eggs of the next generation, all the while looking for food and avoiding becoming someone else's dinner.

Don't imagine that there will be ravening hordes of butterfly caterpillars wrecking the garden. They are highly selective about their food, unlike wide-ranging foragers such as moth caterpillars and fly and beetle larvae.

Prairie and meadow plantings will attract far more butterflies than a grass lawn or even a border of choice hybrids, since many of these overbred perennial beauties lack the nectar that is so abundant in the simple single flowers of the original species. Even if you are not creating a prairie lawn or meadow, it is worth incorporating a few of the species in formal borders and among shrubs.

Buddleia davidii is commonly called butterfly bush and, as if to disprove my statement above about hybrids, the many cultivars of this fragrant shrub will attract butterflies. California lilacs *(Ceanothus)* are also highly attractive to butterflies. *Viburnum* species, staghorn sumac *(Rhus typhina)*, dogwoods *(Cornus)*, and many species of willow

RIGHT *At Great Dixter, East Sussex, England, Christopher Lloyd has been trying out all sorts of extreme combinations of plant; the luscious mauve, pink, and acid green typify the vivid colors he seems to favor. The dull brown of the desiccated thistle provides contrast.*

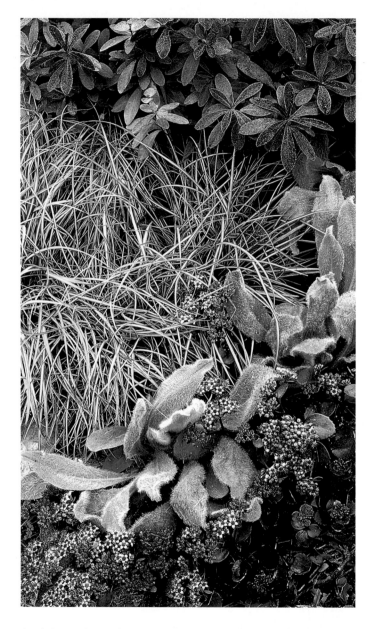

wintering shelter for beneficial insects and butterfly progeny. In the flower garden, among the butterfly perennials that would find a home in a prairie lawn are the New England aster (*Aster novae-angliae*), bee-balm (*Monarda didyma*), butterfly weed (*Asclepias tuberosa*), summer phlox (*Phlox paniculata*), purple coneflower *(Echinacea purpurea),* and *Verbena bonariensis.*

In a prairie or meadow planting, the plants are distributed in broad drifts or colonies among the grasses. This suits the feeding habits of butterflies; they choose their food source by color, and a mass makes more of a show than a single plant. They also prefer to flit from one flower to another rather than lingering over a particular blossom. And in autumn there are plenty of colorful perennials to provide fodder for migrant butterflies.

(*Salix*), and poplar (*Populus*) are all havens for butterfly species. Some of these plants flower in early summer, but the foliage will have something to add to the color of the autumn garden as well as providing the necessary over-

LEFT *Autumn gardens are enlivened by good foliage mixes; perennials like* Sedum *'Vera Jameson',* Euphorbia dulcis *'Chameleon',* Hieracium villosum, *and the sedge* Carex *'Frosted Curls' show what is possible.*

RIGHT *Color and shape contrasts in the yellow-splashed foliage of* Euonymus fortunei *'Sheridan Gold' and a* Rubus *species with chocolate markings.*

FLAMING BORDERS

For many gardeners, flowers offer the greatest creative potential. They are the pigments, textures, and shapes on the horticulturist's palette, from which wonderful pictures can be composed in the beds and borders that make up the heart of the garden.

The gardens of ancient Persia were metaphors for heaven, and in these gardens water features, fruit trees, and scented flowers were combined to create an earthly paradise. In medieval Europe, monastic cloister gardens devoted to the cultivation of herbs and vegetables served the monastic community, while the flowers were grown as altar decoration and for herbal medicines. From these symbolic and practical beginnings, early flower gardens evolved. Roses, lilies, and wildflowers, collected from hedgerows, mingled with exotic shrubs and herbs from the Holy Lands introduced by returning crusaders to decorate the ladies' gardens or "flowery meads" within the castle keep. These intimate, enclosed gardens were

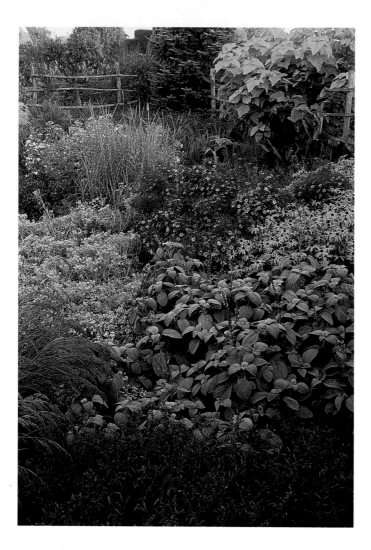

The prominence of flowers in gardens came under attack during the seventeenth and eighteenth centuries. Formal parterres, endless tree-lined avenues, and the principles of the Landscape Movement led by Capability Brown were imposed upon the natural landscape. The woodlands and meadows of England were sculpted into green parks. But flower gardening never really lost its place in the heart of the average man. Grandiose schemes and the novelty of Capability Brown's "landskip" never caught on with the

LEFT *More of Christopher Lloyd's bold autumn planting with* Plectranthus argentatus, Anaphalis margaritacea, Aster *'Little Carlow',* Rudbeckia fulgida *var.* deamii, *and* Miscanthus sinensis *'Strictus'.*

RIGHT *At West Dean, Sussex, England, the autumn borders are filled with plants like* Heuchera *'Palace Purple', nasturtiums, rudbeckias, the favorite red dahlia 'Bishop of Llandaff',* Salvia confertiflora, *castor bean (*Ricinus communis), *and the seedheads of red orach (*Atriplex hortensis *var.* rubra).

PREVIOUS PAGE *Autumn flower borders need not be dull if enough use is made of the huge Michaelmas daisy clan. At Waterperry Gardens, Oxford, England, the borders are filled with multicolored daisies, sedums, rudbeckias, and goldenrod.*
INSET *Purple coneflower (*Echinacea purpurea) *is another autumn warhorse, here surrounded by other seasonal stalwarts like Solomon's seal, bistort (*Persicaria amplexicaulis), *red valerian (*Centranthus ruber *'coccineus'), sneezeweed 'Rosea', and* Helenium *'Kupferzwerg'.*

fenced by simple wood palisades and decorated with turf seats and shady flower-covered arbors. Such flower-filled bowers can often be seen in the background in fifteenth-century manuscript illuminations, allowing us a glimpse of that romantic age. It was a simpler time for gardeners as well—well before the introduction of a whole new world of plants. Beginning with the European discovery of South and North America and increased trade with Africa and the East Indies, the course was set for modern flower garden design.

more conservative land-owning gentry of England, whose gardens proved a refuge for the jumble of cottage-garden flowers that had cheered gardeners for centuries. These were also the people who established and held England's colonies, bringing with them their familiar flowers and gardening methods. Soon they were sending back wonderful new plants to Europe, thereby extending the flower palette and spurring on new developments in flowers and gardening.

For the past fifteen years at least, contemporary English gardening has been dominated by the past; by garden designers' emulating the flower border plantings and cottage garden style of the Edwardian garden designer Gertrude Jekyll. Her influential color theory for combining flowers in long broad borders was first described in 1908, in her book *Color Schemes for Flower Gardens*, which is still in print today. Vita Sackville-West, who created a garden during the 1930s and 1940s at Sissinghurst in Kent, is prominent among the world-famous English gardeners whose planting schemes have been inspired by Jekyll's work.

Planting schemes designed according to these principles depend upon the dynamics of color theory for their impact. But modern designers, perhaps thinking that it is difficult to move forward if you are always looking back, are seeking a new aesthetic, with the result that many contemporary designers and home gardeners are taking a much more ecological approach to flower gardens. Their concern is to establish a balance of nature in their flower borders, rather to strive for an artistic balance of color.

They may have their differences, but one thing uniting Jekyllistes and "Wild" Gardeners is their mutual recognition that autumn flower gardens offer something special. For the former, the hot colors shared by autumn-flowering plants and the long growing season offered by flowering exotics from the tropics and subtropics allow them extended playtime. The latter recognize that naturalized perennials embedded in a matrix of ornamental grasses are at their prime in autumn, as the grass seedheads make a frothy background to the composite and umbellifer perennials and annuals that populate prairie and meadow gardens.

FLOWER GARDEN PREPARATION

When planning a garden, my first move is to chart the passage of the sun and play of shadow around the site at various times of day and over as long a period as I can manage. Sketching in these areas on tracing paper allows me to create a layered map and to pinpoint full-sun hotspots, areas of perpetual shade, where and how far the morning sun reaches, and which areas of garden first fall into afternoon shade—essential information to help identify planting zones. Add to this any observations on areas of moist soil, wet boggy spots, dry arid patches, frost pockets, and wind catchers, and the result is a pretty accurate site profile.

Several conditions will affect the type of flowers you will be able to grow, but many flowering plants will do well no matter where in the garden you choose to place them, as long as the soil is well prepared and the plants receive at least a few hours of sunshine each day. Exceptions to this are plants that require full sun; full shade; dry, free-draining soils; moisture-retentive soils; or combinations of these main characteristics. One quality that effects all plants, no matter what sort of condition they prefer, is the soil pH.

There are a number of soil-testing kits on the market, including gauges you poke into the ground to take a reading. I prefer the most basic technology: a test tube in which you dissolve an indicator tablet in distilled water, then add a half teaspoon of soil. Shake it well and let the soil settle until the water clears. The water will have turned to a color that you then compare with the color chart in the kit. This indicates the level of acidity or alkalinity. As mentioned in the first chapter, neutral (6.5 to 7) is what suits most plants.

I would never recommend trying to amend soil so as to grow acid-loving plants in alkaline soil, or vice-versa. You can make changes, but over time you will find that the soil will revert, or else you will have to make the adjustments every year. I really don't see the point in it. Keep life simple. If you really have to grow some choice lime-hating plant in your chalky garden, then plant it in a container and water with rain water if your tap water comes from wells (chances are that ground water will be alkaline in a chalky area).

All flower garden preparation is done in the autumn, and most of the planting as well. Turn the soil to at least a spade depth, taking care to remove all perennial weed roots as you go. Incorporate pea gravel or sand to loosen heavy soils or add decomposed manure or compost to loose

soils to enhance moisture retention. Even if the garden is intended to be a dry garden, the plants will appreciate this initial improvement of the soil, particularly if you take the trouble to add the compost at a much deeper level than you might ordinarily do. This will encourage the plants to put down deep roots in their search for moisture, and the deep-rooting will in turn sustain them through dry spells.

Hardy herbaceous perennials die back during winter. Their top growth withers and decays completely in frosty weather, or else remains as a burnished skeleton continuing to contribute something to the garden picture. Meanwhile, the crown and roots remain below ground protected by the soil layer and any protective mulching you laid down in autumn. Tender perennials are plants from exotic climates and will not survive winter frosts or freezes outdoors. Except in mild climates, they should be lifted and brought into the greenhouse or other frost-free place and stored in layers of peat moss or dry sand. They can also be propagated from cuttings in late summer and then kept in a greenhouse from autumn until the last frost.

Annuals and biennials also have much to offer the flower gardener, and since they are only passing tenants of the border, can be used to fill gaps while perennial plants are filling out. Hardy annuals complete their growth cycle in one year; from seed sown in autumn to flower in the following spring and early summer, setting seed again by early autumn the following year. Half-hardy annuals also have a shorter cycle; they are generally sown in the spring to flower through into autumn. The seed of biennials is sown in the autumn of year one. The plant establishes a root and leaf system the first year, then flowers in the second. Nursery-grown biennials are often sold in the autumn and can be planted then in their flowering positions in the garden. Winter-flowering hardy annuals like pansies are also on the market during late summer and early autumn.

DESIGNING FOR A FLOWER GARDEN

The main thing to remember when planning is that you are making a garden for your own pleasure, so anything that makes you happy goes. There is enormous pleasure to be had from a carefully constructed polychromatic flower border that builds to a crescendo from the lyrical pastels of early summer to the hot jazz flares of autumn. In my garden at Sycamore Barn, I attempted to arrange the borders by the season, so that the moisture-loving plants of early

spring were against the east-facing, shady side of the garden that didn't seem to dry out so much during the summer. The summer roses and their company of silver-leaved artemisias, lavender, catmint, irises and alliums went along the south-facing, sun-soaked boundary, while the autumn border faced the west and the setting sun and was set against a dark yew hedge that heightened the glow of the autumn colors of Michaelmas daisies, brown-leaved grasses and sedges, and the many prairie plants I raised in homage to my American roots.

Give the plants room to breathe. By that I mean try to make the borders roomy enough to accommodate the planting without looking shoved against a fence or crammed into a corner. If you have a lawn edged with perennial borders, make it proportional. The lawn should provide a setting for the plants rather than being a vast green sea with a few perennials clinging to the edges.

LEFT *Beth Chatto's gravel garden is famous for its collection of dry-loving plants, many of which are at their peak in autumn.*

RIGHT *Grass borders have much to offer the autumn gardener: in the foreground at Upper Mill Cottage the border begins with bright yellow* Hakonechloa macra *'Aureola', blue-gray* Elymus hispidus, Pennisetum orientale, P. alopecuroides, *and* Carex conica *'Hime-kan-suge'. Tall-growing grasses behind are* Miscanthus sinensis *'Flamingo',* Stipa arundinacea *(an excellent grass all year round),* Molinia caerulea *ssp.* arundinacea, Miscanthus sinensis *'Zebrinus' with horizontal yellow bands, and* Stipa brachytricha.

In small backyards, you can get more planting space by laying out the beds diagonally. This way the corners form deep beds around a diamond-shaped lawn. Larger gardens can have informal island beds that break up the space, the grass areas serving as paths winding between the islands. Use lengths of laundry line or rubber hose to help define the curves of an island bed—hose has a helpful habit of curving naturally, so it is easier to use. When you have finalized the plan, grab a can of cheap spray paint and mark out the shapes to be dug.

It is often advised that you arrange plants so that the tallest are at the back of the border or in the center of the island bed, with the size gradually decreasing toward the front or outside—boring. Instead, mix them up, especially when working with autumn-flowering plants in a mixed-season setting. Autumn plants, of any size, can be extremely useful in the foreground, screening the earlier flowering plants as they die back.

If you are going for a color-theme border, you should probably make a working plan to identify exactly which

plants of what color and how many of each you will need. If you are going for a more informal plan, with island beds beneath trees and/or mixed with shrubs, you might be able to work "freehand," assembling the perennials you wish to grow together and arranging them on the garden ground rather as Jackson Pollock dribbled paint onto a canvas—a little here, a little there—striving to achieve a balance of shape and color or piquing interest with contrasting textures and tints.

PLANTING AND MAINTENANCE

Just as for trees and shrubs, autumn frequently offers exactly the kind of planting conditions that are best for setting out perennials: mild, sunny weather, perhaps with a forecast of approaching rain, and a slight breeze to cool you as you work.

Before planting out pot-grown or bare-root plants or lifting transplants, water them well. Soak pots for an hour or so; put bare-root subjects into a bucket of water; drench nursery rows. Once you have done this, begin by putting the plants in their planting places, following your design or instinct. Generally the plants will be container-grown and

LEFT *Flower color changes with the seasons, and in the autumn the shades of yellow, red, and blue are intense, as though they had collected all of summer's sunshine to release in a final blaze of glory. Black-eyed Susan,* (Rudbeckia hirta), *and spiky* Persicaria amplexicaulis *'Rosea' are among the best for color and contrast in autumn flower gardens.*

in plastic pots or bags. Don't remove them until the moment of planting; the plastic protects the roots and prevents them from drying out as you work. Also, you may not complete all the planting in one day, despite your best intentions. If the plants are divisions or rooted cuttings that you have lifted from a border or nursery bed, wrap them in plastic or toss a dampened piece of burlap over the root ball for protection.

Once the plants are set out, try to envision how they will look in full flower: Is there enough contrast between the types of foliage to hold your interest? Will the colors complement each other? Are the contrasts you're trying to create successful? Most importantly, are the plants in the right place, sun lovers in the sun and so on? All your work will be in vain if you haven't suited the plant to the site.

The usual rule of thumb is to plant perennials in groups of three or five or seven, for really large borders and to try to create a fluid transition from one group to the next; Jekyll's plans most often show long "drifts" running obliquely across the width of the beds. At Hidcote Manor in Gloucestershire, England, one of the most famous of Edwardian gardens and the one that had the most impact on twentieth-century English garden design, Lawrence Johnston developed a way of planting a single group of perennial plants or annuals, then a little further down the bed, planting a small cluster of the same plant, then a few feet from that planting one or two more. This gave the effect of a colony of self-sown plants and heightened the natural informality of the garden.

This is a useful way to plant grasses in a naturalistic perennial border, since the effect of natural dispersion is most pleasing and permits you to mesh the various species without its looking too "blocky." Another way to do this is to plant in a series of overlapping circles of various sizes. This is an especially good way to sow seed for annuals or prairie gardens.

BACK TO PLANTING SKILLS

Before planting pot-grown perennials, as with trees and shrubs tease out any roots that are circling around on themselves, trim away any damaged roots, and remove any mossy or lichen-encrusted compost from the top layer of compost around the base of the plant. When using small divisions or rooted cuttings, I have always trimmed the roots by grasping them together just below the base of the plant and clipping away any root ends that protrude from the bottom of my clenched fist. Trimming like this makes it easier to deploy the roots in the planting holes, and small feeder roots seem to develop more quickly from the clipped roots so that the plant establishes faster in its new site. Trim and tidy bare-root plants if necessary (it shouldn't be, if they are from a good nursery).

Make the planting hole large enough to accommodate the root ball and deep enough so that the crown of the plant is just below the soil surface. Put the plant into the hole, fanning out the roots, and then backfill, firming the soil around the roots with your hands as you work. Finish by watering well to help the soil settle around the roots of the plants. If the soil is very dry at planting time, fill each hole with water first and let it soak in before planting. Then be sure to keep the new bed adequately watered for the first few weeks after planting. If it rains, so much the better.

Once the perennials are in place, hardy biennials and annuals can be set out to fill gaps in the young, permanent population. Pansies and violas are especially useful, since they make a cheerful show early in the year and will also help to keep down weeds. Annual plants in perennial borders look most effective in small drifts, so this is a good time to use the Hidcote planting technique. It will help the annuals appear naturalized among the perennials. The final plants to add are bulbs, followed by any annual seeds you may be using. Try to keep bulbs in large clumps, not dotted singly here and there—a clump makes more of an impact when in flower. Spring-flowering bulbs and perennials are best kept to the back of the border or behind later flowering plants, to disguise their fading flowers and foliage.

In addition to using the circles method to sow annual seed in beds and borders, you can draw curving furrows or seed drills in and around the perennial plants. When the seed is sown, lightly rake the soil over the seed and tamp it down with the head of the rake, then water using a fine rose on the watering can (you don't want a drenching

RIGHT *The soft plumes of the pampas grass,* Cortaderia selloana *'Sunningdale Silver', are especially fine and make a good foil for the brighter blooms of* Sedum *'Herbstfreude' and bright pink autumn cosmos, a long-blooming annual.*

ABOVE *Plants with distinct markings set the theme for an associa-*
tion: Sedum *'Stewed Rhubarb Mountain' has fine coloring, with*
dark red stems and mottled pink flowerheads, accenting the varie-
gations of surrounding plants, including Fuchsia magellanica *var.*
molinae *'Sharpitor', and variegated horseradish.*

RIGHT Persicaria amplexicaulis *'Rosea' with tufted hairgrass*
*(*Deschampsia cespitosa *'Goldtau') and the prairie plant Joe Pye*
*weed (*Eupatorium purpureum *'Atropurpureum') make good*
companions; all enjoy the same growing conditions of well-drained,
deep soils.

shower to wash the seed away). Unless you are especially
skilled at sowing, it will be necessary to thin the seedlings
once they have established their first true leaves. Remove
the weakest of the seedlings, leaving enough space between
the remaining ones to allow for healthy growth. Overcrowd-
ing causes disease and weak growth as the plants compete
for nutrients.

Top off the newly planted bed with a good blanket of
mulch—anything from clean, dry straw to well-rotted leaf
compost. Mulch will prevent winter rain from compacting
the top layer of the soil, prevent frost from penetrating the
soil and heaving newly planted perennials out of the
ground, and suppress weed germination in spring. (It used
to be the custom to use peat moss as mulch, but this is not
good ecological practice—it takes millennia for a peat bog
to develop and only decades to strip it bare. Many other
sources of compost are not threatened with depletion; use
something other than peat for mulch.)

Some tall-growing perennials require staking to keep
them from falling over their shorter neighbors. Probably the

least obvious supports are twiggy branches placed around the clump of plants. The tops of the twigs can be snapped to bend over the crown of the plants and as the plants gain height they will gradually conceal the supports. Other methods, such as bamboo canes, wire circles, or crutches are hard to disguise, and least successful of all is a plant girdled by garden twine and tied to a stake, like some sacrificial victim. Put supports in place during autumn, after you have cut off any dead top growth. It will be impossible to do this effectively once the plant is actively growing.

During autumn, established perennial beds should be weeded and lightly dug over to loosen the topsoil. Use a three-pronged cultivator for this task or a small fork to work in the close quarters between established plants. Working the soil will open it up if it has been compacted by rain or baked by the summer sun to a hard crust. Air and moisture can then reach the roots. A dressing of bone meal mixed into the topsoil around each plant is beneficial.

DEAD-HEADING

The removal of dead flowers is not strictly confined to autumn but is something that can carry on all year. It will in many cases help to prolong the attractiveness of a perennial planting. As perennials mature they begin to open up, becoming taller, leaner, and often unkempt in overall outline. By removing faded flowers and cutting back to where healthy new shoots are emerging, you can tighten up the whole picture—somewhat like pulling it back into focus—so that the bed or border continues to look appealing at the end of the season.

Some of the faded top growth of early midsummer-flowering plants can be cut back, and certainly anything

that looks unsightly should be removed. When most flowers fade, they begin to produce seed. This can have a detrimental effect on foliage, which starts to look rather shabby as the plant's functions shift energy into seed production. Perennials valued for their foliage are most likely to look shabby. Not every seedhead is suited to dried flower arrangements and some are just plain unattractive, adding nothing to the garden. But many ornamental grasses retain their looks well into autumn. Umbelliferae and some of the Compositae also have fine seedheads, even if, like the Michaelmas daisies, they are not still actively flowering. So be restrained in your autumn housekeeping: leaving seedheads is one way to have winter interest in the garden.

In cold climates, some less hardy perennials will be protected by their faded top growth, which serves as a loose mulch; Mexican giant hyssop, Peruvian lily, Russian sage, and most of the Mediterranean herbs are plants that may appreciate the winter mantle their faded stems and leaves provide.

Dead-heading is something to reserve for the end of the day; it is quite relaxing to wander through the garden, carefully clipping away individual faded flowers with sharp shears or scissors. Don't go around yanking dead blooms

LEFT *Color contrasts in autumn flowers from the purple umbels of* Allium senescens *ssp.* montanum *var.* glaucum *and the sprays of the fine yellow-flowered* Crocosmia × crocosmiiflora.

RIGHT Crocosmia *'Star of the East' with* Berberis thunbergii *'Harlequin'.*

from the stalk, take the time to cut back to a leaf node; buds forming at that point will be the next flush of flowers. On perennials that have sprays or clusters of flowers, cut away the entire stalk, reducing it by at least half or a third of its height to encourage more bushy growth to develop.

Some plants, like lady's-mantle and hardy geraniums, are difficult to dead-head because the faded flowers are too closely engaged with the foliage. But take a look at the base of the plant and you'll see new shoots emerging, so just cut the old leaves and flower stalks back to just above the new growth. It will soon give a fresh flush of leaves and blooms for late-season glory while disguising the stubble.

Other perennials bloom in a single flush and look dishevelled the rest of season. Use long-bladed shears to remove the dead flowerheads and to clip them into shape; rue, sage, lavender, and catmint fall into this category (although you can cut catmint right down to the ground and get a second blast of blue flowers for autumn).

RIGHT *One of my all-time favorite gardens was designed by Mark Brown for the Cabot Perry garden of the Museum of American Impressionism at Giverny in France. Taking the flora of the hills behind the village, Mark has woven an intricate carpet of grasses, herbs, and flowering shrubs for a garden on a south-facing site that is fairly dry and sun baked. Although lovely all year long, it reaches its finest moment in the autumn, when the soft biscuit tints of the many grasses such as* Stipa gigantea, Sesleria albicans, *and* Brachypodium sylvaticum *are dotted with sweeps of blue flower from salvia, Russian sage, eryngo, catmint, clary, hyssop, and cupid's dart. This exquisite garden perfectly captures the essence of the Impressionist garden, painted with the colors of nature as nature herself might have mixed them.*

ABOVE *Grasses are the ultimate autumn border plant, perfect "binders" for flowers and other foliage plants. Cultivars of eulalia grass* (Miscanthus sinensis) *are among the best, as this border in another Mark Brown–designed garden shows. From the front, there is* M. s. *'Nippon',* M. s. *'Flamingo', a stand of* Coreopsis tripteris, *and the tall-growing species itself,* M. sinensis.

RIGHT *The feathery pink-tinted plumes of* Stipa arundinacea *are among the most tactile of the grass flowers and this particular stipa is hard to beat. It makes a beautiful mound of soft green-gold that blends well with plants like* Yucca filamentosa *'Golden Sword' and the yellow-leaved shrubby honeysuckle,* Lonicera nitida *'Baggesen's Gold'.*

Many tall-growing perennials can be "stunted" to prevent them from becoming leggy and overly awkward. In early summer, after they have a couple of feet of growth, shear them back by a third, or more if you want to considerably reduce their stature. It will make the plant stouter, as well as shorter, as it regrows and will delay its flowering period.

PROPAGATION—DIVISION

There are several methods of propagation for perennial plants, but the easiest is division. And with few exceptions—namely grasses and silver-leaved plants—autumn is the best time of year for this task.

Perennials grow from the center, putting on new growth around the outside edge of the clump. As the clump matures, the center can die out or become weaker, producing less foliage and fewer flowers. Consequently, most perennials grown in conventional beds and borders benefit from being lifted and divided every three to five years.

Water the plant you are going to divide several hours before you start, then use a spade to dig around the periphery of the plant and cut through the roots. Then lever it out of the soil with a fork. If the plant is a clump-forming perennial, and the clump is the size of a dinner plate or larger, stick two garden forks back-to-back into the center of the clump and then pull them apart; this should split the root ball. These smaller clumps can be further divided into smaller planting-size pieces. Pull them apart by hand or tease them apart with a hand fork. The main thing is to aim for several growing points on each clump and enough roots to support new growth. Tuberous-root perennials or rhizomatous plants can be cut up with a sharp knife—just be sure that there is a healthy growing point on each piece and a few root nodes.

Many bulbous plants, like montebretia, alliums, and so on, produce offsets, small bulbs that form around or at the base of the parent bulb. These tiny bulblets can be rubbed off, often with a tiny root attached, and planted. They will usually produce flowering plants in two years.

When they do, cut the stem to divide it into separate plants, place them in pots, and allow them to grow for at least one year before you plant them in the ground. This method also works with lilies that form small bulblets along the stem, such as tiger lilies.

ROOT CUTTINGS

Oriental poppies (*Papaver orientale*) are among the plants that can be increased by root cuttings. In fact if you ever try to transplant an oriental poppy you will never be able to move it entirely; any piece of root left behind will grow a new plant. Others like this are artist's acanthus, bleeding heart (*Dicentra spectabilis*) and ligularia. Generally any plants with stringy roots can be raised using this method.

Lift a clump of the parent plant, remove a well-rooted section and replant the parent. Select lengths of root that are

LEFT *Designer Mark Brown's* Miscanthus *garden shows the tall-growing ornamental grasses to best effect across the broad expanse of unmown meadow.*

STEM CUTTINGS

Some plants, like species of *Sedum*, produce stubby shoots in their leaf axils, the point where the leaf attaches to the stem. These infant plants can be encouraged to root by cutting the entire stem, trimming off the flowerhead, and laying the stem in a box of sandy compost. Cover the stem with a layer of moist compost and put the box in a coldframe or sheltered spot. The plantlets will form roots.

RIGHT *Constance Kargére has introduced some stunning combinations for year-round interest in the double borders that frame the entrance to her family home, Bois des Moutiers, in Normandy, France. Gertrude Jekyll apparently provided plans for entirely impractical annual borders for the Lutyens-designed house. Constance has the same fine eye for color as Jekyll but a more practical sense of planting. Here she has used Japanese barberry (Berberis thunbergii 'Rose Glow') with a claret-red dahlia.*

at least ¼ inch in diameter and cut them into pieces 2 to 3 inches long. Dip the pieces in a fungicide solution, and then lay them in a box of moist, sandy compost. Cover lightly with more compost and water well before placing in a coldframe or greenhouse. By the following spring, new plants will have formed and each can be potted separately.

STRATIFICATION

Establishing prairie or meadow gardens may take many more plants than you would wish to purchase—a good reason to grow your own from seed. Many of the perennial plants used for these gardens require a period of exposure to cold, moist conditions before they will successfully germinate in the spring. Columbine *(Aquilegia)*, monkshood *(Aconitum)*, and the many coneflowers, rudbeckias, and other prairie natives respond well to this treatment.

Seed can be sown in early autumn in small pots, seed trays, or flats or in specially prepared seedbeds outdoors, in a mix of half coarse sand and half fibrous potting mix. Label the pots and trays and place them in an open coldframe in a sheltered, preferably north-facing spot in the garden. Keep them moist; if the compost dries out, water lightly. The seed will not germinate all at once; some may take up to a year to sprout, while others will leap into life. As and when the seed sprouts, move the containers to a spot where they will receive indirect light. Setting them on gravel or coarse grit will help to deter slugs and snails, or use your usual slug bait to protect the young seedlings.

As the seedlings fill out, transfer them to individual containers or nursery rows covered with cloches or floating fabric mulch until they are settled in. Then let the young plants develop until autumn the following year, when they can be planted in the ground.

If you need to sow seed earlier, or if your climate is too mild to provide the winter chill needed, place the seed in small pots and store in the refrigerator for at least six weeks.

NATURALIZING GRASSES

In the first chapter I talked about prairie lawns and meadows as alternatives to conventional grass lawns, and at the start of this chapter about the move towards more naturalistic perennial borders that are modeled on the way plants form communities in the wild. To my eye, these plantings offer the greatest autumn interest and, in fact, make winter gardening something to seriously consider. I have never really believed in "Winter Gardens," preferring to stay indoors when it is cold and anticipate the arrival of the first spring bulbs. My skepticism was reinforced when my friend Sally sent me a photo of her winter garden in Boston. Everything was hidden by a deep blanket of snow; it could have been shrubs or dustbins beneath the lumpy white shapes that dotted her small garden.

Contemplating a matrix of fine-leaved grasses on a snowy day changed my mind: The beauty of grasses such as the eulalia *(Miscanthus sinensis)* cultivars 'Gracillimus', 'Morning Light', 'Kleine silberspinne', and 'Undine'; species of stipa like *Stipa tenuissima* or *S. arundinacea*, and switch-grass, *Panicum virgatum*. Snow does not seem to build up on their narrow leaves, and in the case of eulalia especially, the flower stems remain fairly stiff and do not double over under frost or snow. These grasses keep their form pretty well; their skeleton stems stand tall above the drifting snow and their wispy foliage rustles in the winter chill. Other cold-weather structure grasses are Ravenna grass *(Saccharum ravennae)* and some of the ever-blues (they appear more blue than green!) and bronzes, like blue oat grass (*Helictotrichon sempervirens*) or the eye-catching bronze leather-leaf sedge *(Carex buchananii)*.

These are clump-forming grasses, and most of them are very tall indeed—Ravenna grass is like a refined pampas grass and can reach up to 12 feet in height, while the sedge makes bristly clumps about 2 feet tall. To ensure they have enough space to grow elegantly they should be planted at least as far apart as they are tall; in a mixed group, be guided by the tallest plant. Use the very tallest grasses as signature plants, and treat other sizes as you would other flowering perennials, creating drifts from the smallest and significant groups or

ABOVE *Zinnias are particularly fine annual flowers that are at their best from late summer to first frost.*

clusters from medium-size ones. Mingle herbaceous perennials among the clumps of grass—purple coneflower *(Echinacea)* among the pinkish, caterpillarlike plumes of fountain grass *(Pennisetum alopecuroides),* or yellow-flowered black-eyed Susan *(Rudbeckia hirta)* among the brassy green of *Stipa arundinacea.*

Most grasses will be container grown, so they can be planted at any time of year, although the general practice is to plant in the spring. However, I have successfully planted in autumn, and this is useful if you're incorporating herbaceous perennials in the scheme. It is an unbroken rule that all division and transplanting be done in spring when the grasses are again growing strongly.

Plant grasses exactly as you would any other perennial. Add some bone meal to the backfill to give the grass something extra to work with as it settles in. Once the plants are established, there is no need to feed. But pay attention to watering and do it regularly during the first year as new roots are put out. Then, as with feeding, once the plants are established most will be fairly drought tolerant.

Grooming grasses is important to help maintain vigor as well as appearances and should be done in late winter or early spring. *Miscanthus* and other grasses that die back should be cut down to within 6 inches of the ground. Others that are evergreen or semievergreen can be "combed" with a rake to remove dead foliage and flower stems.

Perennials that carry their flowers on long stems, or ones that have trailing, scrambling stems, work best with grasses. Many of the best are autumn-flowering, daisy-type plants from the Compositae family. Michaelmas daisies offer a huge range of color and flower size to choose from, and there are several sorts of coneflower, including the white-petaled *Echinacea purpurea* 'White Swan'. The goldenrods *(Solidago),* have plenty of interesting yellow-flowered family members of varying heights (from 1 to 5 feet) and habits—from the rigidly upright *S. rigida,* which has erect stems up to 5 feet tall topped with fluffy

yellow pompons, to *S. rugosa*, which has a wide spread of arching stems bearing clusters of bright yellow flowers along their tips.

Sedums flower in autumn and are valuable for their ruddy tints and unusual colors of foliage, ranging from the red of *Sedum telephium* 'Matrona' to the variegated green and white *S.* 'Gooseberry Fool'. Japanese anemones, or windflowers, have a stalky upright habit that mingles well with clumpforming grasses. Phlox and *Verbena bonariensis* are other good upright perennials to use among grasses.

Foliage contrasts that work well with grasses can be found among members of the Umbelliferae family. The erect stems and saucer-shaped flowerheads among this group of plants also work well with clumping grasses. Fennel, myrrh, dill, Queen-Anne's-lace, wild and cultivated carrot, angelica, and even parsnips are all part of this family

LEFT In England, Beth Chatto has, through the example of her show gardens in Essex and her many fine books, encouraged gardeners to suit the plant to the site. While it may be possible to amend the soil, making it more acid or alkaline to suit whatever it is you want to grow, the amendment will not endure and will have to be repeated periodically to keep the plants healthy. It makes more sense to work with what you have. Observe the conditions of your soil, the amount of light or shade the planting zone receives, and the moisture levels, and plant accordingly. In dry shade, few things do better than groundcovers like epimediums and periwinkles; they also provide an excellent background to the autumn-flowering colchicums, disguising the latter's faded foliage.

and have the characteristic ferny foliage and lacy white flower clusters. But some of the umbellifers have attractive purple foliage, like the biennial herb *Angelica gigas*, or the delicate dove-gray form of cow parsley, *Anthriscus sylvestris* 'Ravenswing'.

Eryngiums are thistlelike umbellifers and the leathery leaved sea holly, *Eryngium maritimum*, has a good dense gray color. Its relative, *E. bourgatii* is tinged with blue, while *E. × zabelii* has the bluest flowers and bracts of all.

One of the chief delights of having grasses in the garden is the beauty of their seedheads. However, with some species the seed can all too readily self-sow, as I found with tufted hairgrass (*Deschampsia caespitosa*). This is one of the loveliest grasses for autumn and winter interest, with dark green glossy foliage topped by a cloud of flower panicles that fade to soft golden brown in winter. But it seeds in a frenzy, and soon a seething crowd of juvenile plants popping up throughout the border. Of course, it is easy to weed them out (and then pot them to pass along to other gardeners, with a warning about its invasive nature, of course), and this is probably the best way to deal with free self-sowers. Rather than try to decapitate the plants and lose their autumn glory in the process, stay on top of the weeding to keep the population in check.

AUTUMN BULBS

In her 1936 book, *Adventures with Hardy Bulbs*, the American garden writer Louise Beebe Wilder gave a good definition of what it means to naturalize bulbs: "In its narrow sense, to naturalize bulbs means merely to plant them in an informal and unstudied manner in contra-distinction to their use in formal beds; but in the broader and more accepted sense, it means to broadcast them on a generous scale in woods, in meadows ... on rough banks or about the outskirts of the garden, to suggest, as best we may, nature's handicraft, not man's."

The most effective way to give a naturalized appearance is to plant bulbs in masses or in clusters of one variety so that it seems as if a self-sown or mature group has spread under its own impetus over the years. Although bulbs for naturalizing are fairly rugged characters, they do best where competition is not too fierce, so avoid planting at the base of shallow-rooting trees or shrubs or in areas where there is thick groundcover or thick turf. In lawns and grassy meadows, select areas where the groundcover is sparse or thin. Peel back flaps of sod, lightly dig the exposed soil, and then scatter a handful of bulbs across the surface. Replace the sod flap, and tamp it down. The bulbs will come through the grass easily.

Autumn crocus, properly known as colchicum, is not really a crocus. Colchicums are especially good at naturaliz-ing and will rapidly form a substantial colony. Plant them along a woodland edge or amid the perimeter plants of nat-uralized perennial beds so that their dishevelled appearance during spring and summer is camouflaged. These bulbs are sometimes called "naked ladies," because the autumn flower appears without foliage; this appears in the spring and dies away—untidily—during summer.

ABOVE *Colchicums grown with petunias is another of Christopher Lloyd's bright ideas—very bright in fact. These charming autumn bulbs are rarely associated with other flowers, doing their time in horticultural purdah wherever their ungainly foliage won't be too obvious.*

RIGHT *Cyclamen, however, enjoy a devoted following and are encouraged to naturalize where they will.*

Crocus speciosus is a true crocus that flowers in autumn. It gradually makes a colony of millions of tiny bulbs that produce delicate violet-blue flowers quite early in the autumn, amid a thicket of narrow green leaves. These little flowers look marvellous in orchards where the grass grows weakly in the shade of the fruit trees.

Cyclamen have always held a special appeal for me; their tiny little winged flowers pushing proudly up through a blanket of autumn leaves is enormously encouraging. The foliage too is extremely attractive, and the ivy-leaved cyclamen, Cyclamen hederifolium, has wonderful foliage marked with silvery veins. The larger the corm the bigger the leaves. They do best in light shade and loose sandy soil among shrubs or with other small-stature perennials. The corms have little hairy roots protruding around their girth, and the young leaves will be tightly curled at the crown. Plant them in small colonies about 4 to 6 inches apart, with the crown is just below the surface of the soil. Cyclamen self-sow; you can collect the seedlings to transplant and enlarge the colonies, or you can collect the little round seedpods. Sow the seeds in trays of sandy compost after soaking them first to aid germination.

Among the countless spring- and summer-flowering bulbs, the alliums offer the best hope for the autumn garden by virtue of their uncommonly attractive seedheads. Allium cristophii is deservedly popular for the starry little purplish flowers that form a large cluster atop the rigid stalk. These dry perfectly well in situ and look terrific among autumn grasses. A. schubertii needs a little protection to survive a mild winter, but the flowerhead is at least 18 inches across, and like A. cristophii it dries into an eye-catching ball of spiky stars.

Curiosities like these, combined with flower-garden stalwarts, are what make autumn gardens lively and interesting. They pique our interest and make the hard work of autumn garden chores worthwhile.

HARVESTING
THE GARDEN

While I admit to a childlike enthusiasm for misty days and
kicking up piles of autumn leaves just to hear their dry
rustle, it is the mellow fruitfulness of the season that really
gets me worked up. All those ripening pumpkins, ears of
late sweet corn as succulent as chunks of honeycomb;
beets, chard, crisp romaine, tangy endive, and crunchy
Gravenstein apples plucked from the bough are enough to
make one forget the fraught moments of drought, pests,
and disease that so often accompany the summer gestation
of all this autumn bounty. It's a good thing too, or we'd
never know the thrill of a homegrown tomato or the clean
bite of a freshly harvested onion. Riches indeed.

As a place to begin learning about gardening, you could
hardly do better than to sow a row or two of annual vegetables. Add a couple of perennials like rhubarb or artichokes, a
gooseberry shrub, and an apple tree and you will have
experience with each major garden plant group. And then
you get to eat the results! Furthermore, all the important

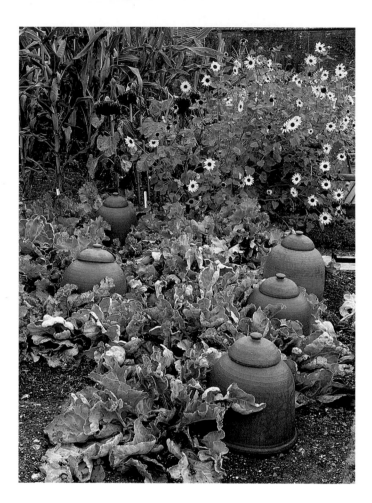

or compost and fertilizer. This is traditionally how vegetable gardens are managed and how I began raising vegetables—until I discovered raised beds.

Already popular in the United States and Europe in the early 1980s, in Britain raised beds were then a novel approach—and caused a few raised eyebrows down at the allotments where I exercised my new skills. In 1988, I wrote of the wonders of raised beds in *The Art of the Kitchen Garden*. This method allows you to fertilize, cultivate, water, and generally focus your energy on only those pieces of ground that are used for growing. Pathways separate the beds, and these are left untilled, but not exactly unloved since they must be kept as weedfree as possible.

To construct raised beds, mark out the areas to be dug. These should be no more than 4 feet wide, so that the middle of each bed can be reached from the side, and as long as you want. Make paths between the beds 1 1/2 to 2 feet wide;

garden tasks assigned to autumn also happen in the kitchen garden: digging, sowing, planting, cutting back, cleaning up, composting—what have I left out?

The basics of digging are described in the introduction; in the kitchen garden the technique is no different if you follow what I have always called "flat earth" methods, when the vegetable garden is tilled in its entirety, like a microversion of a farm field, turning in a blanket of muck

LEFT *Bright red terracotta rhubarb forcers and late sunflowers decorate a functional space.*

RIGHT *Apple cordons trained along a wire fence divide this traditional vegetable garden.*

PREVIOUS PAGE *Even brussels sprouts are attractive additions to the garden if you grow an ornamental variety like this 'Rubine' with its purple-tinted foliage.*

INSET *Highly visible in the autumn kitchen garden, the ornamental lemon cucumber adds bright spots of color.*

they can be paved, gravel, grass (which must be mown regularly) or mulched with woodchip, straw, or other inert material. Edge the beds if you like, or simply bank and firm. The beds are "raised" by the extra-deep layer of well-rotted manure and compost that is added to the bottom of the trench. This technique requires copious amounts of the best muck you can get.

As always when digging, work methodically, from one end of the bed to the other. The first trench of soil you remove should be dumped at the end of the bed where you will dig the final trench, and used to backfill. The finishing touch is to tidy round the edges of each bed, making a narrow gutter between the path and the bed and firming the gently sloping raised sides.

Once the beds are established, the compost is added to the top layer and lightly forked in. Because the beds are never walked on, the soil is not compacted and so is better aerated, this makes routine digging unnecessary. The openness of the soil means that it warms earlier in the year, so crops can be sown sooner, and that the fertility is high, so they can also be grown closer together. In the spring, rake the surface to a fine texture and get sowing.

COVER CROPPING

In the autumn as a bed is cleared of its crop, you can make a late-season sowing of an overwintering crop or dress the bed with a layer of rotted manure or compost, which is beneficial to both gardeners and earthworms. These creatures will thank you for the food source by taking the

manure down into the soil, an action that is really good for improving heavy soils. Alternatively, sow a "green manure," a leafy, quick-growing crop.

It is important to not leave soil bare between crops; rain can wash away valuable nutrients, erode the beds, and create a hard, compacted surface. A green manure crop however, takes the nutrients into its developing structure of leaves, roots, and stems to later be released back into the soil when the crop is dug into the beds and then decomposes. The growing crop protects the soil surface and when dug in becomes a valuable soil conditioner. There are green manures to suit most garden needs: Some are deep-rooting

ABOVE *Thistle flowerheads are at their best in autumn and are especially valued by flower arrangers. This is* Carlina acaulis *bronze form.*

and draw nutrients from the lower soil levels that are released as the crop's foliage decomposes; others draw atmospheric nitrogen to their roots, where bacteria convert it to a form that will supplement present levels of soil nitrogen.

Overwintering green manures that protect the soil and prevent the leaching out of nitrogen are sown in autumn; among the best for this purpose are winter vetches and field beans (*Vicia sativa* and *V. faba*), crimson clover (*Trifolium*

incarnatum) and common rye (*Secale cereale*). In the spring, to condition soil before sowing late autumn and winter crops, use fiddleneck *(Phacelia tanacetifolia),* the herb fenugreek (*Trigonella foenum-graecum*) or buckwheat (*Fagopyrum esculentum*). Buckwheat and fiddleneck are quite pretty, with white and blue flowers respectively, and are also attractive to bees. Clover cover crops are natural habitats for ladybugs; they feed on the aphids that are attracted to the clover and the ready food source encourages the ladybugs to mate and lay eggs. The emerging larvae then shelter in the clover foliage.

Raised-bed gardening, with its geometric form and system of pathways, is akin to the highly desirable historic "potager" garden, where flowers, fruit, and vegetables are grown together in an edible landscape design. Integral to this idea is the concept of companion planting, a growing partnership where flowers, vegetables, and fruit are planted together to their mutual benefit, generally as a natural means of pest control (garlic with roses to keep aphids away) but sometimes to promote healthier growth otherwise (datura with pumpkins). The use of companion planting as a benign method of pest control was recognized centuries ago, when households relied on "strewing herbs" to keep vermin levels down. Lavender, sweet sedge, sage, tansy, and hyssop are just a few of the plants whose branches and leaves were scattered on the floor to deter fleas, lice, and so on. In French, the word *garde-robe* was the common name of southernwood, *Artemisia abrotanum;* its pungent foliage was used to keep moths out of linen cupboards. Translate this to the kitchen garden and use fragrant herbs to protect vegetables.

One of the most popular and widely used floral pesti- cides is the marigold (*Tagetes*); along with other potent- smelling plants it can be used to edge or partner vegetables, disguising their scent, while the marigold's roots secrete a chemical that soil nematodes find repellant. Insects find their food source by scent and shape; one of the cleanest rows of carrots I ever grew was between rows of onions interspersed with pot marigold *(Calendula officinalis)*. I like to think that the carrot fly couldn't smell its favorite food, but maybe it just couldn't see it! It has been discovered that weed-free plots with widely spaced, neat rows stand a greater chance of infestation by insects that rely on sight to find their food source: A tidy row of cabbages neatly outlined against immaculately hoed soil stands out like a billboard to passing aphids and whiteflies.

Many beneficial insects will be attracted by the pollen or nectar flower companions can offer. For example, hover- flies like to sip nectar, and hoverfly larvae feed on aphids. So intercropping with companionable plants and the close row planting that raised beds support are beneficial on many levels.

INTERCROPPING

Travel is a garden lover's best teacher; by exploring other people's gardens we can learn new techniques, discover new plants, and generally broaden our horticultural horizons—a sort of intellectual intercropping, sowing the seeds of some new idea beneath the protective mantel of proven practice. For example, in England raised beds are good because in a wet climate, they drain more freely. But a visit to Bahrain showed me how to deal with the hot dry conditions I now contend with in Texas. Instead of raising the beds I will sink them to form water-retentive reservoirs that can be period- ically flooded beneath a protective straw mulch.

More literally, intercropping means making the most of the vegetable garden space by sowing a fast-growing crop along with a slower, longer-standing crop. I first saw inter- cropping in practice in Italy, in a typical rural *horto* of the sort that seems to occupy any space of open ground ("if it's empty, plant it" is the motto there). In a small household garden, the grapevines had been trained into a sort of low, sheltering arbor, tomato plants climbed canes fixed between each vine, and cabbages grew at their feet, shading the roots of the taller plants. The garden was pretty to look at, simple in its application, and economic in it uses.

Leaf crops like lettuce and spinach can be sown in suc- cession among onions, garlic, leeks, beans, beets, turnips, and other crops that take some time to reach maturity. Brassica crops do well when interplanted with dill and fennel, and I especially like the autumn-harvest look of pumpkins and squash crops growing between rows of sweet corn. This takes up a lot of space, and if you have it, try it. The pumpkins do well with the regular watering corn receives.

RIGHT *Elder is a common hedgerow shrub or small tree, and the shadowy tint of* Sambucus nigra *'Guincho Purple' is especially seductive. Elderberries make a tangy jelly and can be part of the blend for hedgerow wine, made only in the autumn.*

A WORD ABOUT EARTHWORMS

Earlier, I described the symbiotic relationship between earthworms and gardeners. Like digging, they are essential to gardening; in fact, they are nature's diggers. I read some amazing statistics to the effect that each earthworm turns a ton of soil a day and that without their recycling action of dragging vegetable and other waste into the soil to aid decomposition, our world would be waist high in unsavory detritus in the time it takes to say "knife." So let's hear it for earthworms.

I must own up that even though it gives me a rush to see a healthy population churning away in my compost heaps, I still find it's kind of creepy to touch them! Nonetheless, this autumn I built a wormery. The restricted space of my new Texas garden, doesn't allow enough room for the usual compost heap. Instead, I have a plastic garbage can that has been punctured all over by drilling holes in the sides and has large drainage holes cut in the bottom; it sits in a shady corner. Red wrigglers, the compost worms *par excellence*, can be bought, although they may already live in the garden and could emigrate. About 1 pound of worms per bin is sufficient.

Just like a compost heap, a wormery is filled in layers, alternating vegetable kitchen waste, annual weeds, other

LEFT & RIGHT *Trees laden with ripening apples and pears are a heartwarming sight, and with their mouth-watering colors they make an attractive element of a mixed border, although they are more often confined to orchards.*

MEANWHILE, BACK IN THE KITCHEN GARDEN...

In her groundbreaking book (an unavoidable pun, I'm afraid) *Creative Vegetable Gardening*, Joy Larkcom clearly and vividly sets out everything you could possibly need to know about how to make a kitchen garden. She is particularly lyrical on ornamental vegetables—the ones that are showy enough to make it into the flower garden—and several of these are especially useful to carry interest through autumn and well into winter throughout the garden. Foremost among these must be 'Rhubarb' Swiss chard. Few vegetable plants are easier to grow from seed, and a row sown several weeks before the last frost will give you clusters of ruby-stemmed plants to spice up foliage groups in beds and borders or to accent the potager. Chard doesn't respond well to transplanting, so raise plants in small pots in a cold frame to plant out with as little root disturbance as possible.

Ornamental cabbages are familiar stock in garden centers among trays of winter pansies and other seasonal flowering plants—and rightly so, since the foliage is difficult to beat for color: from rich vinous purple to pure white, with all shades of red and glaucous blue-green in between. The leaves are often very finely cut, like a neck ruff of Flanders lace in a painting by Van Dyck, or broad and spreading with heavily frilled edges. I have often seen these planted out in evenly spaced rows of bedding—a not very inspired use of something better treated as an eccentric and planted in loose groupings amongst other strongly colored plants. Red-leaved mustard greens and giant curled mustard

reasonably soft waste with layers of worm bedding, which can be anything: garden soil, shredded newspaper, straw or sawdust litter, or autumn leaves (run the mower over the leaf heap a few times to shred it coarsely). Be sure the bedding is evenly moist before adding it—in a 50:50 ratio—to the waste. I exclude animal-derived waste of any kind and only add grass mowings a little at a time. I'm eagerly anticipating my first harvest of wormcast compost, which is guaranteed to be the best soil conditioner going.

greens are ornamental in the same way and ideal for warmer climates where the cabbage might struggle.

Amaranth is another annual flower or vegetable, depending on how you care to use it. The foliage of leafy Chinese amaranth has purple markings suffusing the center of each leaf, while 'Red Stripe' is, as you might imagine, red along the central vein. Sow amaranth in bold patches and harvest it to eat like spinach. Grain amaranth, on the other hand, has tassel-like flower plumes that come in shades of bright yellow, dusky bronze, green and dark mahogany red. The renowned Dutch plantsman Piet Oudolf grows a 5-foot-tall bronze form of amaranth as an ornamental plant in perennial borders.

Even chili peppers offer some fiery autumn colors, as well as flavors, of course. In gardens in the southwestern United States the tiny little pequín pepper can be seen casting its incendiary ruby red beads over rocks and through grasses. I've been told that they register more than 30,000 Scovilles (the unit of measurement for chili heat)—increasing my admiration for the Mexican gardeners I know who munch them by the handful with their lunchtime tortillas.

LEFT *Remember the glory of glossy red currant beads. This is 'Red Lake'—they can add a sassy glimmer to shrubberies or a sharp tang to fruit glazes on pies or in preserves.*

RIGHT *Hedges will often be overrun by blackberries. In the kitchen gardens their snaking rampant canes can be controlled by pruning and training against wire supports.*

Rocambole or top-set garlic, leeks, onions, and other "vegetable" alliums have a delightful flowering habit, making flower buds on the tips of the leaves, each one wearing a pointy little cap that is doffed as the flower bursts open. Artichokes and cardoons have some of the finest "architectural" foliage in the plant kingdom. They make stately plants up to 5 feet tall, with broad, gray felted leaves that are divided like an acanthus leaf (also a favorite ornamental for the autumn garden). Red-leafed orach is an old standby

LEFT *Figs are worth growing for the shade cast by their distinctive leaves and the fragrance redolent of warm Mediterranean evenings, as well as for their sweet fruit.*

RIGHT *The grapevine* Vitis 'Brant' *produces juicy purple berries that are highlighted by the rich autumn color of the foliage.*

with claret-colored leaves. However, it and bronze fennel will seed lasciviously, and once they take on height are hard to pull out, so think of your back muscles and weed out ill-placed plants before they take you out! Shiso *(Perilla frutescens),* is another dark-leafed vegetable that is often used as a bedding plant to provide a background to showy annuals. One of the most startling bedding displays I ever saw incorporated cardoons, red chard, brown and parrot-green grain amaranths, and red-leaf sweet corn. It was outlandish but succeeded because it was done with such flare and conviction. Look through a good vegetable seed catalog and you'll discover a world of decorative edibles from which to create your own unique autumn vegetable show.

AUTUMN FARE

One of the most vivid portraits of the art and craft of vegetable gardening was painted by the American comic genius, S. J. Perelman, in his series of articles for the *New Yorker* titled Acres and Pains. Anyone who has ever bought a "place in the country" or entertained visions of home-grown produce swelling the larder, and waistline, should read these achingly funny essays, which describe Perelman's experiences as a landowner in rural Bucks County, Pennsylvania, during the 1940s. Let me share with you his take on the summer harvest, arrived at only after much expense, "untold agonies," and encounters with man-eating snails:

"By the end of August the residue left by the rabbits and woodchucks is ready for harvest. It is always the same—tomatoes and squash. [They] never fail to reach maturity . . . Soon the most casual acquaintances start dropping in with creaking baskets and hypocritical smiles, attempting to fob off their excess tomatoes and squash. The more desperate even abandon tiny bundles on our doorstep like infants at the House of the Good Shepherd. The kitchen becomes an inferno, and the wife a frenzied sorceress stirring caldrons of pink slush . . . The only solution is to plow everything under and live on pie."

As someone who has toiled more hours than she might wish over steaming pink slush and had tons of squash and tomatoes rejected at the orphanage door, I can tell you in all honesty that the only options are to go cold turkey and toss tempting seed catalogues into the bin the moment they arrive, or resolve to grow less—much less—or sow smaller quantities of more varieties. Do you really need such a long row of squash plants? Also, with some things it seems that no matter how carefully you organize the sowing calendar, religiously making successive sowings of lettuce or spinach at biweekly or longer intervals, chances are they will all be ready at once. However, we know that our resolve will weaken, so let's make the harvest a good one by taking care to pick when the crops are at their prime. Fruit and vegetables in good condition are the best to use for preserving and freezing—and eating.

Water is crucial to the successful growth of crops, so water well and regularly—and in the morning if you use a sprinkler or overhead watering system, since overnight moisture can encourage mildew and other blights. A soak or drip hose laid along the raised beds is a good way to ensure adequate, economical watering. The water goes directly where it is needed, and considerably less water is lost through evaporation. The bulb-forming vegetables, from garlic to turnips, will grow more quickly and be more succulent if watered well; sweet corn, zucchini, eggplant, pumpkins, and melons also require lots of water throughout their life cycle. Conversely, too much water after fruit sets causes grapes and tomatoes to crack and strawberries to be squishy and flavorless.

As they begin to mature, check regularly that potato tubers and carrot tops are adequately covered by soil, and if necessary draw up extra soil along the rows, since exposure to sunlight causes the vegetables to turn green and green potatoes are poisonous. When onions, shallots, garlic, and potatoes are ready to harvest, do not water for a week. Lift them on a warm sunny morning; gather potatoes as soon as the soil is dry and doesn't cling to the tubers. Turn onions up and leave on the top of the soil so that the sun can dry the roots and base of each bulb before bringing them in.

Peas, beans, summer squash, and pickling cucumbers will continue to flower and be productive if regularly picked; otherwise the plant starts seed-making and production shuts down. Most vegetables taste better when harvested young: beets the size of golf balls, carrots only as big as a finger, zucchini the moment the flower drops off (or pick the flower to eat deep-fried in light tempura batter), and glossy green snow peas that are little-finger size. Gather fresh beans before the pod gets bumpy, but leave dry beans to mature on the vine.

Sweet corn fanatics insist that the best time to harvest is the when the water is boiling—so that the fresh ears can be dropped instantly into the cooking pot. This is not so urgent now that there are hybrids that keep their sugar longer before getting starchy. Generally the ear is ripe when the tassels turn brown and the sap from a punctured kernel runs milky white rather than clear.

Apples, tomatoes, strawberries, raspberries, plums, okra, and melons are ripe when they literally fall into your hand when touched; they should not have to be cut or pulled. Sweet peppers, brussels sprouts, and rhubarb should be gently twisted to separate them from the plant.

HARVEST FAIR

The harvest festivals that have been celebrated since the dawn of settled agrarian civilizations, acknowledge the handing over of power from Flora, the goddess of spring and summer flowers, to Ceres and Pomona, the goddesses of agriculture and fruitfulness. In rural England, before the Industrial Revolution and the mechanization of farming, it was the custom at harvest to dress the final wheatsheaf and to cut and braid and ornament it as a "kirn baby" or "corn dolly," representing the spirit that was thought to dwell in each ear of wheat. And because it was bad luck to be the person who made the final cut, thus supposedly killing the last of summer's bounty, the reapers would take it in turn to swing their scythes as they worked the field, mowing down the standing grain together, so that no single person would be cursed with ill fortune. Today, village harvest festivals are usually centered on floral displays in the parish church, and it is a great time to stock up on homemade jams and fruit

RIGHT *A shaded walk planted with hazel trees is a marvelous sight. In spring, soft green tassels hang down from the shadowy branches and on breezy days you can watch the pollen float from tree to tree, ensuring autumn's crop of hazelnuts.*

preserves, cakes and pies, made by the villagers and sold at the fairs and bazaars that are part of harvest time.

In Britain, corn dollies are made from clean straw that is braided into intricate patterns, with the grain-bearing ears of wheat topping off the doll like a golden crown. I recall the corn dollies from my Illinois childhood, which were made from the broad flat leaves left after shucking the ears of corn bought by the bushelful from roadside stands. And then we made corncob pipes for bubble-blowing contests using soapy water—that weren't particularly successful.

Other festivals also mark the passage of autumn, and Michaelmas, or St. Michael's Day, is the next important one to be celebrated. An antique poem describing the calendar in terms of the seasonal flowers introduces autumn thus:

The Michaelmas Daisies, among dede weeds,
Blooms for S. Michael's valourous deeds;
And seems the last of floures that stode,
Till the feste of S. Simon and S. Jude —
Save Mushrooms, and the Fungus race,
That grow till All-Hallow-tide takes place.
Soon the evergreen Laurel alone is greene,
When Catherine crownes all learned menne,
The Ivie and Holly Berries are seen,
And Yule Long and Wassaile come round again.

St. Michael was known in the ancient Celtic Christian church as Michael nam Buadh, the conquering angel who cast the Devil into Hell. The myth continues that the Devil landed first in blackberry bushes, and in rural counties it was said that the Devil had stamped on the fruit and that it was extremely ill-advised to gather blackberries after Michaelmas, September 29. The Michaelmas goose was usually the centerpiece of the festive table, served with autumn vegetables, cabbage, leeks, and parsnips, and decorated with roast-spiced apples.

As autumn turns to winter, so the souls of the dearly departed were thought to return to earth to warm themselves at the hearth fires of their loved ones and to partake once again in the love and community they had enjoyed while alive. But it was not just the good ghostly spirits of friends and family that returned; also goblins, witches, frights, and haunts revisited the earth to wreak mischief and havoc. I remember staying as a child at an aunt's house in the Kilkenny countryside around the time of Halloween. In hushed tones she warned me that not only would the leprechauns be out and about that night but the fairies would be running through the countryside trying to lure the unwary to follow them into the hills with promises that their life's treasure would be revealed. Those that were gullible enough to follow were never seen again! (In other words, be grateful for what you have here and now.)

Native to the New World, the bright orange jack-o'-lantern pumpkin had yet to be discovered when folk started making ghoulish faces on hollowed-out turnips to scare away goblins and witches. The tradition of trick or treat harks back to the idea of placating evil spirits with offerings of food and drink, like the bowlfuls of oats and milk placed on the doorstep to satisfy the hunger of returning spirits. However, All Souls' Day, which falls on the second day of November also had a tradition of "souling," when the poor were permitted to beg door-to-door for alms in the way that the unhappy souls of the dead returned on that day to seek solace among the living.

In Celtic tradition, November 1 marked Samhain and the return of winter. Bonfires were lit to symbolically fend off the coming chill. On November 5, in England, more bonfires are lit to mark Guy Fawkes Night, when an effigy of the man who tried to blow up the Houses of Parliament is burned atop a huge bonfire. On November 11, in France, the feast of Martinmas honoring St. Martin, the patron of beggars and outcasts, is celebrated. People carry candle lanterns through the darkened houses and streets, symbolizing the light and hope brought by St. Martin.

Finally, the cycle of autumn festivals concludes with Thanksgiving Day, celebrated on the fourth Thursday of November wherever there are Americans and they can roast a turkey. This unique holiday has, wherever it is observed, introduced one of America's greatest desserts to the culinarily deprived of the world—pumpkin pie! Love it or hate it, it's more American than apple pie, and twice as filling.

Before I began raising delicate little sugar pie pumpkins in my English garden, I had to depend on canned pumpkin purchased at huge expense from the food hall at Harrods department store in London. Growing pumpkins has become something of a cult as British gardeners have come to recognize the a huge variety of shape, color, and flavor

ABOVE *The ruby red hips of* Rosa rugosa *'Scabrosa' appear in early autumn while the shrub continues to throw plenty of bright pink, spicy-scented flowers among the golden yellow autumn-colored foliage. Rose hips can be used to make a sweet jelly or syrup that is rich in vitamin C, and a jelly made of apple and hips flavored with savory herbs like tarragon or thyme makes an especially fine condiment to serve with roast meat or poultry.*

among pumpkins. In France and Italy there are several pale-skinned varieties with mild, sweet-flavored flesh. The vast, flat, deep orange 'Rouge Vif d'Etampes' resembles the pumpkin Cinderella used to get to the ball and is used to make the delicious *potage au potiron*, a classic of Orléanais cuisine. A dove-gray type is extremely popular in New Zealand and Australia, where, friends tell me, pumpkin is the national vegetable, appearing regularly on every barbecue.

HARVEST SOUP

In October, the field pumpkins return to the roadside stands, waiting to be selected for jack-o'-lantern carving. It's great fun searching for the Perfect Pumpkin, and even more fun eating the soup that can be prepared from the flesh once Halloween is over. I make this soup by cutting the vegetable into large chunks, peeling them with a sharp knife, tossing them in olive oil, salt, and pepper, and then roasting them in the oven until soft enough to pass through a food mill, which is preferable to using a food processor. The purée will be silky smooth. An alternative to roasting is to steam the pieces in a microwave oven to conserve the flavor and texture.

In a large saucepan, soften a large chopped onion and one large clove of garlic in about 2 tablespoons of butter. Add one tablespoon of white wine to moisten before pouring in 2 cups of chicken stock. Simmer a few minutes before adding 4 cups of puréed pumpkin. If the mix is too stiff, add more stock or wine to thin it to the preferred consistency. Season with salt, pepper, and one teaspoon of toasted and ground cumin seeds (toast the seeds in a

dry frying pan until the aroma is released). Sprinkle with chopped fresh cilantro before serving.

While researching recipes for *The Art of the Kitchen Garden*, I came across a pie recipe in an English cookbook of 1685 titled *The Accomplish't Cook*, written by Robert May. This is a savory rather than a sweet pie, in which the pumpkin is coarsely chopped, mixed with eggs, and flavored with thyme, rosemary, and marjoram, as well as cinnamon, nutmeg, and cloves—which in the seventeenth century were very expensive spices. The mixture was fried and then layered in the pie crust with sliced apples and raisins over which a custard of egg yolks and white wine was poured to bind it all together as it baked. Judging by the exotic spices and the complexity of the recipe, pumpkin must at one time

ABOVE *Pumpkins and other winter squash are among the most colorful and decorative denizens of the autumn garden. Pumpkins are the mascot of the season, for making jack-o'-lanterns in October, pumpkin pie in November, and warming soups and pastas dishes during winter.*

have enjoyed a certain popularity, probably because of its novelty value as a New World import. But the basic mixture, with or without spices (and leaving out the raisins and apple), bears a reasonable resemblance to the traditional filling for *Ravioli di Zucca*, pumpkin ravioli. The best pumpkin to use for this would be the Antipodean gray-skinned type, as it is firm and has a lower water content than others. Sage goes well with pumpkin, too, and is part

of the traditional Italian recipe, as is a handful of grated parmesan cheese.

PUMPKIN PIE

The classic sweet pie mix is a custard made by combining 3 lightly beaten eggs with 1 cup of sugar, 1 teaspoon of salt, and mixed spice. Scald 1 cup of milk and $^{1}/_{2}$ cup of heavy cream. Stir it slowly into the egg mixture, and then add 1 cup of puréed pumpkin. Blend well until evenly mixed, pour into a prebaked 9 inch pie crust, and bake at 400°F for the first 10 minutes, reducing the heat to 325°F for a further 20 to 25 minutes, or until a knife inserted in the middle comes out clean. The pie filling will crack and brown around the edges, and the center will be glossy and slightly tacky to the touch. Serve à la mode, with generous scoops of real vanilla ice cream. Forget the turkey and trimmings!

KNOW AND LOVE YOUR SQUASH

Pumpkins are just one sort of winter squash, and all squash are members of the Cucurbitaceae family. It is a huge group that includes the familiar types like zucchini, acorn squash, and little flying-saucer-shaped pattypan squash with their crimped edges, as well as the weirder crookneck squash, butternut squash, spaghetti squash (steam in the microwave and serve with fresh tomato sauce), and warty-skinned Hubbard squash. Summer squash are eaten in summer (surprise!) when the skin is soft and the fruit immature; winter squash are eaten from autumn through winter, since they are mostly hard shelled and so can be stored. Some winter squash have extremely hard skins, but if you cut along the "seam," or longitudinal ridge, you can generally gain access to the flesh and the seeds. Incidentally, don't throw away pumpkin seeds. Roast and salt them instead; they are very nourishing. Soak them first in water for about an hour to release them from the gooey fibers.

Baked acorn squash is delicious prepared with 1 tablespoon of butter and brown sugar nestled in the scooped-out middle; any squash can be prepared this way, or roasted as described for pumpkin. Serve roasted pumpkin with a balsamic vinegar dressing as part of a *salade tiède,* or warm salad. In her book *Chez Panisse Vegetables,* Alice Waters gives some of the best winter squash recipes, including one for risotto made with a chicken stock base and diced butternut squash flavored with sage and white wine and finished with parmesan and butter. Leave the finished risotto in the covered pan for 10 minutes before serving to let the flavors blend.

PRESERVES, CONSERVES, AND KEEPING THE HARVEST

One corner of my grandmother's basement in Milwaukee, Wisconsin, was lined with Kilner jars and earthenware crocks filled with apple butter, sauerkraut, bread and butter pickles, bottled beets, mustard beans, and other comestibles that she produced from her regular harvesting of the farmer's market, downtown. She was not a vegetable gardener herself, although she grew her own dill and chives and some other herbs. Her expertise was in the kitchen, and anyone who could make a cabbage taste that good was expert indeed. But because I choose to grow my own, the conserving of the harvest must be reduced to a minimum. I rely on the microwave and the freezer. If it freezes—and most vegetables will—I first slice, dice, or otherwise prepare the vegetables, and then zap them on high in the microwave for about 3 minutes, about 8 ounces at a time, with just the water that clung after cleaning. Spreading the vegetables in an even layer in a shallow dish and covering them with a special microwave dish cover seems to work very well. But it is critical to transfer the vegetables to a large bowl of very cold water the moment they come out of the oven. This stops the cooking process so the flesh doesn't become mushy. Then drain them completely to prevent ice crystals forming. To freeze, spread them on baking sheets or special freezer trays, then bag and label them when they're frozen. This way, you can cook as much or as little as you like later, and the vegetables will cook quicker and more evenly than they would in a solid brick.

To deal with the tomato glut and avoid hours of stirring steaming pink sludge, you can microwave or roast the harvest. Cut each fruit in half and scoop out the watery seeds in the middle. Pack them in a single layer in a nonstick baking pan, and put it in a hot oven until the cut edges begin to brown. Let the roasted tomatoes cool before purée-ing them in a ricer or food mill; the pulp will pass through,

RIGHT *Drying flowers for decoration is one of autumn's more pleasing tasks.*

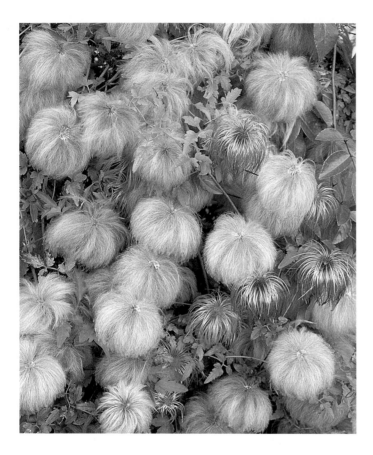

but the skins will be left behind for the compost heap.

Sweet corn can be frozen the moment it is picked, husks and all. It is cold work removing the outer leaves later, so wear gloves. You'll find the silk comes away easily.

HERBAL HARVEST

The kitchen garden is not the only place where autumn's bounty can be found; many herbs are highly ornamental plants, and now is the time to gather in branches of rosemary, thyme, tarragon, marjoram, and other shrubby herbs. Some

herbs, like thyme and marjoram, can be cut back to bristly clumps; tarragon can be shaved to the ground.

Some care must be taken with rosemary; in cold climates the plant needs some protection for its branches.

Tie the branches you've gathered together in small bundles, or spread them over a drying rack made by stretching cheesecloth or muslin across a wooden frame. Leave the herbs in a shady spot where the air circulates freely to dry slowly and evenly. Under the bed can be a good place (if you are dust conscious and keep that area clear!). Otherwise, hang the bunches from an indoor clothesline. I have dried rosemary and thyme successfully in the microwave by putting the branches on a paper towel to absorb the moisture that is given off, but be careful not to burn the herbs. Remember that they have oil in their leaves.

Soft-leaved herbs like parsley and coriander dry less successfully in my experience, so to have "fresh" green leaves on hand, I rinse them in clean water, shake off the excess, and put in freezer bags. The leaves will shatter the first time you scoop some out, but it's rather like having instant chopped herbs ready to flavor stews and soups. You can also freeze chopped herbs in stock: Place a teaspoon or so of the herb in each section of an ice cube tray, and then fill the tray with

LEFT *Seedheads are among the bounty of the autumn garden. The silky seedheads of* Clematis orientalis *are among the best.*

RIGHT *The emerald pods of agapanthus last well in the border and look good among ornamental grasses.*

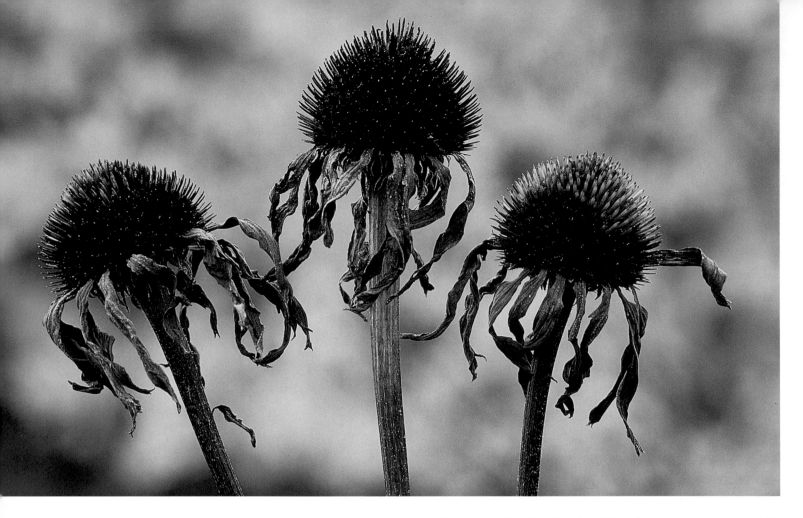

ABOVE *Some seedheads are particularly dark and distinctive, like those of the purple coneflower.*

RIGHT *The dark tones of angelica umbels and the seed-bearing whorls of Jerusalem sage* (Phlomis fruticosa) *are silhouetted against pale plumes of the grass feather reed grass* (Calamagrostis acutiflora 'Karl Foerster').

fresh stock. This is better than using plain water since the addition of a frozen herb cube won't water down the dish you are preparing.

This is also a good way to conserve pot marigold (*Calendula officinalis*) petals. The bright yellow marigold petals were known as the poor cook's saffron for the bright coloring they impart to a dish and the warm, softly spicy flavor they lend to broths. Next time you poach or coddle an egg, sprinkle a few calendula petals over the top; the white will color as if saffron threads have been added.

POTPOURRI

Marigold petals dry very well for use in the kitchen or in potpourri, one of the oldest dried flower concoctions still in use today. Lavender and rose petals are the main ingredients in potpourri, which translates as "rotten pot"—so called because the earliest mixes were moist with perfumed oils and kept in covered jars. The lid would be removed to release the scent and to top up the mix with fresh petals as needed.

Other flower petals used are violet, heliotrope, mignonette, sweet woodruff, and pinks. The foliage used is predominantly citrus-scented, like lemon verbena, lemon balm, and any of the scented-leaf geraniums. Boxwood leaves and kitchen herbs like rosemary, thyme, and sage fill out the mix and the perfumes are preserved by stirring in a blend of cinnamon, nutmeg, whole cloves, mace, and violet-scented orris root powder, which is prepared from the dried root of the Florentine iris. Essential oils are added too, a few drops now and then. Patchouli and sandalwood lend a seductive note, while flower oils make a lighter scented potpourri. Salt is used to make a moist potpourri, as it prevents mold and stops the petals actually rotting down to an odoriferous compost—use coarse sea salt or kosher rock salt.

Gather flowers in the morning just after the dew has dried from the petals, and spread them to dry as described for herbs. Have ready a large earthenware crock with a lid or other container with a tight-fitting lid. Add the flowers and foliage in layers with the salt and the spice–orris root mix. To a pound of flowers and foliage add roughly 2 ounces of orris root and a tablespoon of each spice. To make a moist potpourri, add 3 to 4 ounces of salt mixed with the spices of your choice between 1/2-inch layers of flower and foliage. Leave the potpourri tightly sealed for ten days, then decant it into a large bowl and mix well.

I have a huge bowl of potpourri to which, over the years, I have added flowers and leaves from our garden and from the bouquets my husband has given to mark, so far, each of the twenty years of our marriage. The bowl serves up my life story in a way, brimming as it is with love and memories, to be added to with scented leaves and flowers from my Texas garden.

SAVE A SEED, SAVE A PENNY

Cottage gardeners were frugal gardeners; not for them the yearly purchase of expensive packets of hybrid seed. Instead, they left a part of every crop, be it vegetable or flower, to ripen on the stem and provide them with the wherewithal for next year's harvest. Following in their tradition can save you a few pennies as well as add a wealth of texture and shape to the autumn garden.

As I have already mentioned (on occasions too numerous to list), don't rush to tidy up in autumn. Instead, take the time to mark the flowers that really knocked your socks off and the vegetables that were especially good to grow and eat. Tie a tiny string around the plants so you know which flower to aim for, and as the seed ripens keep an eye on it to gather in the capsules before they burst. Of course, this will only work if the seed you are earmarking is from species plants or old-fashioned, "heritage" plants—garden forms that have not been the subject of hybridists' improvements. (I'm not convinced that a grossly double, pompon holly-hock or poppy is necessarily more desirable than a simple old-fashioned single, where each part of the flower is clearly defined and the color shines true and bright.)

LEFT *Let your autumn garden go to seed. It's what the season is all about, and you will be rewarded with some pretty effects and plenty of self-sown seedlings to pot and share with fellow gardeners. Here, wooly betony* (Stachys byzantina *'Cotton Boll'*) *displays showy, fuzzy spikes against a background of fairy wands* (Dierama pulcherri-mum), *and baby's breath* (Gypsophila paniculata *'Schneeflocke').*

There is no hard-and-fast rule about when seed is ripe for gathering, it is simply a case of look and learn. Some seed capsules literally explode when the seed is ripe; among these are dill, caraway, fennel, hardy geraniums, and euphorbias. So keep an eye on the plant, and when the pod begins to darken, snip it from the plant with a length of stem intact and put it into a paper envelope. Label it clearly, and then set the envelopes in a dry, warm spot. The pod will ripen and spit its seed into the container.

On legume pods—including lupines and sweet peas as well as beans—wait until the pod looks like the shell has been shrink-wrapped around the seed inside. Then gather them up, set them somewhere to dry for a few days, and then shell the seed just as you would shell beans.

Martagon lily pods and iris pods tend to split open, exposing the seed, and then slowly unfold until wide open. Gather the seeds before the breeze catches the papery lily seed or birds peck out the iris seed, depositing them naturally as they are digested.

Some seed comes with feathery attachments or chaff that is hard to separate from the seed; other seed is just plain painful to gather, like thistle or coneflower seed. For the latter, put the entire dried flowerhead in a paper bag and wait for the seed to drop out naturally. You can gently roll it around to help the process. Don't bother to remove the chaffy bits if you are going to sow the seed in your own garden, the seed will germinate anyway. But if you are going to barter the seed, clean it up first.

THE LASTING
FRAMEWORK

The snow-covered lumps in my friend's Boston garden could be said to be adding shape and form to the winter garden scene, just as the shapes and textures of the shrubs and trees supporting the snow make the autumn view of her garden more interesting. It is not just the color of foliage or the brightness of the flowers that make the autumn garden a beautiful sight to behold, it is also the contribution they can make as boundaries, eye catchers, screens, and sculpture that define the garden throughout the year, as well as being of major significance in autumn and winter.

HEDGES

Gardens are not natural; one of the most obvious changes a gardener makes to the natural terrain is planting hedges, which apart from prehistoric earthworks are probably the oldest artificial feature in the landscape. Hedges defined the perimeters of villages and individual properties and separated vegetable gardens from the stockyards. Most often hedges were planted using saplings scavenged from the wild or grown from wild-gathered seed. One of the earliest descriptions of hedge planting details how it could be easily done by impregnating a length of twisted hemp rope with the seed of hedgerow plants. The rope was laid in the trench where the hedge was needed and then watered well and regularly. It was kept weed free, and seedlings were quickly established. Traditionally, hedges were planted beside ditches; the owner of the ditch owned the hedge, since the soil for the ditch was thrown back onto his property, and the hedge was planted on top of the mounded soil.

My garden in rural Norfolk was bounded on two sides by a hedge that was at least 150 years old. There were magnificent crab apple trees (great for making herb jellies in autumn), bullace plums, holly, hazel trees, elders, and field maples. Throughout the year the hedge was vibrant with flowers, fruit, birds, rabbits, foxes, owls, and numerous butterflies and other beneficial insects. There was also one old apple tree of a variety called 'Arthur Turner' that was still producing huge cooking apples, but with old age its yield was gradually lessening.

With a backdrop like that against which to plant a garden from scratch, I was bound to use the ancient hedge as the leading inspiration for any new hedge planting I undertook. Ultimately I had a mix of hedges that divided a large unruly cottage garden into specific planting areas. There were clipped linear evergreen hedges in dwarf

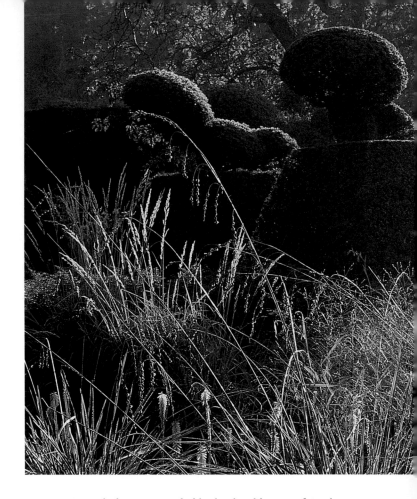

ABOVE *Peacock shapes are probably the the oldest motifs in the art of topiary. This is the Peacock Garden at Great Dixter, East Sussex, England.*

PREVIOUS PAGE *At the gardens at the Old Vicarage near the North Sea coast of Norfolk, England, strictly disciplined hedges divide the garden into distinct rooms. Most importantly, they provide much-needed shelter and help create the microclimates the extensive plant collections need to survive. The perfectly clipped topiary reinforces the vistas and ornaments the avenues of this extensive formal garden.*

boxwood around a small formal lawn and an eight-foot-tall yew, a sweeping curve of midnight green that separated the ornamental flower garden from the wilderness of orchard and hazel tree walk beyond. The tall hornbeam hedge around the formal flower borders gradually became a mixed

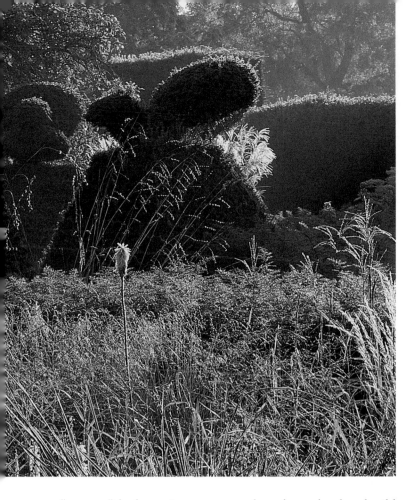

"tapestry" hedge as it came to enclose the orchard and wild garden areas. Near the house were hedges of sweet briar and rugosa roses to scent the evening air, along with lavender and catmint. In their maturity, the garden hedges matched the character of their setting and the garden benefited from the protection that the field hedge gave the beds and borders.

Incidentally, a tapestry hedge is one which is made up of all sorts of different hedging plants. In England, the most famous tapestry hedge is at Hidcote Manor Gardens in Gloucestershire, where the creator of the garden, an American expatriate, used a blend of hollies, yew, boxwood, and hornbeam to divide the garden into a series of rooms, each quite different in character from the other. One of the best times of year to visit this garden is in the autumn, when the hedges are turning and the foliage and flowers present a marvelous selection of seasonal color.

PATIENCE IS A VIRTUE

I firmly believe that the biggest mistake people make when planting a hedge is to use "fast-growing" shrubs. It is false economy. Lawsons cypress is especially evil, as I know from personal experience. The builder who converted the old barn into a house planted a mixed bag of these fast-growing evergreens. I always meant to dig them out, but never got around to it. At first I thought the fact he had planted them in their black plastic pots would be enough to kill them (always let it be said, "Remove pots before planting"), but I had not bargained on the tenacious grip these things had on life. Away they grew, and the more I trimmed and topped (which I admit was infrequently—there being so many other things to do) the larger and faster they grew. Now they are the new owner's problem, and I am truly sorry.

However, I am now doing penance with the hedges around my Texas garden. The previous owners shared with many American gardeners the inclination to plant something evergreen around the house. So I have acquired an unhealthy blend of privet, Burford holly, and aphid-covered euonymus, all planted smack up against the foundations, which I'm sure isn't what the well-known U.S. landscaping feature called "foundation planting" is meant to be.

I know it to be a myth that evergreens like yew and boxwood are slow growing, which is the reason gardeners usually give for not planting them. The yew in my English garden was a 25-foot curve of luscious dense green that reached its height of 8 feet just seven years after planting.

It regularly put on 18 inches of growth in the first few years and then slowed to 10 to 12 inches in later years, because once it was established and growing well I stopped feeding it. And I did not begin the hedge with 4-foot-tall plants, but rather 2-foot-tall rooted cuttings, which were considerably cheaper. Other yew hedges in the garden were raised from seedlings transported from the yew grove at a friend's property in Kent. These seedlings were also about 2 feet tall and soon caught up, thanks to regular feeding and watering. Similarly, the dwarf boxwood hedging started out as fist-size, rooted cuttings planted on 1-foot centers. I have to admit that it took me a few seasons to believe that they were actually growing, but within five years they had knitted together to form a dense frame for the formal lawn.

It is no secret that if you water and feed, the plants will grow. My regime for the yews and box was to feed with a quite high-nitrogen fertilizer in the early spring, just as things were beginning to wake up. (Pelleted chicken manure or, if you can get it, Peruvian bat guano is best.) Then I took care to water well throughout the summer, applying a general-purpose, balanced fertilizer in mid-summer. The same regime worked for the hornbeam hedges and the tapestry hedge, while the lavender and roses received a general feed during summer and were mulched with rotted compost along with the rest of the garden.

Late summer and early autumn is the time to prune and clip yew hedges and most deciduous ones; take care to clip so that the hedge is wider at the base than at the top. In the first few years the aim is to create shape and bulk; after that you must remove the new growth to retain the shape and prevent the shrubs from outgrowing the confines of the desired height and girth. (My inherited hedges are scraping the gutters, but I'm told things are supposed to be bigger in Texas.)

KNOTS AND OTHER CLIPPINGS

Patterns made of lightly clipped dwarf hedges, planted with colorful flowers or filled with colored stones, have the appearance of oriental carpets laid on the garden ground. Frank Lawley, who is an expert on oriental carpets and one of England's finest plantsmen, has a theory that such carpets indeed inspired this decorative garden device. Knot gardens were hugely popular during the Tudor period. Henry VIII had a huge collection of oriental carpets, some "inherited" from the ill-fated Cardinal Wolsey, while others were no doubt purchased from Venetian tradesmen who were importing these fabulous textiles from Persia and the Orient. Portraits of the period often show oriental carpets in the background, so it seems a quite natural extension to take the motifs, translate them into hedge and flower, and spread them in the garden below the best rooms of the manor house or palace. During every season of the year, the knot would give something pleasing for the eye to rest upon.

Contemporary knot gardeners can use abstract motifs to create the pattern or fall back on traditional designs. These are easily found; a number of gardening books over the past ten years have included plans and details, including my own book *Herb Garden Design*. There are two basic forms of knot: Lawley's knot garden is an open knot; the paths that cut through it allow you to walk on the floral carpet. Closed knots are ones where the pattern can only be viewed from outside the knot.

Knots are ideal for small courtyard gardens where formality is required. The small beds formed by the interweaving hedges can be planted with bulbs, annuals, and perennials to allow a varied display throughout the year. It is standard practice, too, to clip the shrubs before they flower, which has always seemed a pity to me, since the lemon-curd yellow buttons of *Santolina pinnata* ssp. *neapolitana* 'Edward Bowles' are quite pretty; and all the herbs flower prolifically, attracting bees and butterflies to decorate the knot. So, ever the iconoclast, I never pruned my knot (described below) until the early autumn, by which time it was looking distinctly unknotted. However, that to me is part of the charm of autumn gardens.

Edging boxwood (*Buxus sempervirens* 'Suffruticosa') has been the plant of choice for most knot gardeners over the years, but gardening texts from the sixteenth and seventeenth centuries list herb shrubs like hyssop, rosemary, thyme, lavender, and southernwood as possibilities for knot-planting. In Italy during this time, small flowers like the lawn daisy were popular for laying out temporary patterns, while pinks, sea thrift, and other clumping groundcovers were also popular. In my Norfolk garden, I had, in addition to the boxwood lawn edging, a knot of sorts; it was more free-form than based on any historical model and planted with hyssop and the evergreen

Santolina rosmarinifolia framed with gray-leaved southernwood. In his Northumberland garden at Herterton House, Frank Lawley has planted a physic garden using pink-flowered *Saxifraga* 'Clarence Elliott' to edge the central beds of the herbal knot, while the side beds are framed with white-flowered sea thrift. Were I to plant a knot in my Texas garden (perhaps using a lasso or half-hitch as a motif?) I would be tempted to try dwarf yaupon holly combined with 'Tuscan Blue' rosemary and the excellent 'Sawyers' lavender.

Knot gardens planted with perennials can be tided up in autumn and mulched to give a neat appearance during winter. If you are going to bed out the knot for seasonal interest, clear away the summer show to make way for bulbs and winter-hardy annuals.

TOTALLY OVER THE TOPIARY

Tudor gardens must have been incredibly lively to look at, what with all the knots, mazes, and gilt, and polychromatic garden ornaments that decorated the space. In the background of a portrait of Henry VIII's family is a small glimpse of a garden, complete with raised flower beds edged with narrow rails painted in green and white diagonal stripes and garnished at the corners with wooden sculptures of the King's Beasts (unicorns, dragons, etc). These are painted white, red, and other pure colors and highlighted with glittering gold (also present is one of Henry's oriental carpets). It is said that these sculpted ornaments are what inspired early English topiary: geometric and figurative shapes clipped in boxwood and yew. Another thought is that Crusaders, having seen peacocks and other oddities in the Near East, embellished their manor gardens with shrubby representations of the exotica they had encountered. This sounds just about as fanciful as the topiary itself.

Like a hedge that lends structure to a dormant garden during the late autumn and throughout winter, topiary shapes provide a visual anchor in the landscape, although some might say "blot," as I discovered in 1987 when researching *English Topiary Gardens*. It seems there is no gray area with topiary—people either love it or hate it. William Robinson, author of *The English Flower Garden*, was a hater; in his scheme of things—wild and natural gardens—topiary was an abhorrent aberration. Topiary had been around a long time before Robinson's time, at least since it featured in early Roman gardens in Italy and its outposts (including Britain), and it may well predate that by some millennia—there are representations of clipped trees in ancient Egyptian papyri. But topiary really reached a zenith of popularity in the Arts and Crafts gardens of Edwardian England, and soon

LEFT *Clipped boxwood and holly define the knot garden beds at the Old Vicarage. Each bed is filled with bold-colored annual flowers and foliage that carries the garden through to first frost.*

RIGHT *A simple pot filled with the spiky gray foliage of clove-scented pinks draws the eye toward the planting behind, where* Aster novi-belgii *'Winston S. Churchill' and A. 'Coombe Fishacre' mingle with the 'Helga' dahlias and little blue flowers of Chinese plumbago.*

spread to the Colonial Revival gardens of the eastern United States. In Europe, and wherever Italianate gardens were built, topiary would be incorporated into the miles of boxwood edging that created the garden rooms.

Because of its artificial nature, topiary is most often found in formal gardens, reinforcing the architecture of the garden with a design vocabulary that includes tetrahedrons, spheres, cones, pyramids, peacocks, teapots, and teddy bears. Such shapes mark the corners of informally planted herbaceous borders or divide the planting space of herb gardens into spoke wheels and sheltering bays. Wherever zoomorphic topiary appears, it is usually the result of a fertile imagination let loose on an innocent boxwood tree. "That branch sticking out just seemed to suggest a peacock tail," or "The hedge had got rather lumpy, and began to look like the Loch Ness Monster," are how two gardeners once described their inspiration to me.

Just as autumn is the ideal time to plant a hedge, hardy shrubs destined to be topiaried should be also be planted now. Because the shrub or shrubs will be in place for a very long time, they will be making extra demands on soil fertility, so prepare the ground generously, incorporating plenty of well-rotted compost or manure and making sure that the drainage is adequate. If the soil is very heavy, add gravel or sand; compost will improve the water-holding properties of sandy soil.

When purchasing boxwood and yew plants for hedges, knots, or topiary, in the case of cutting-raised material, try to buy ones that have been raised from the same stock.

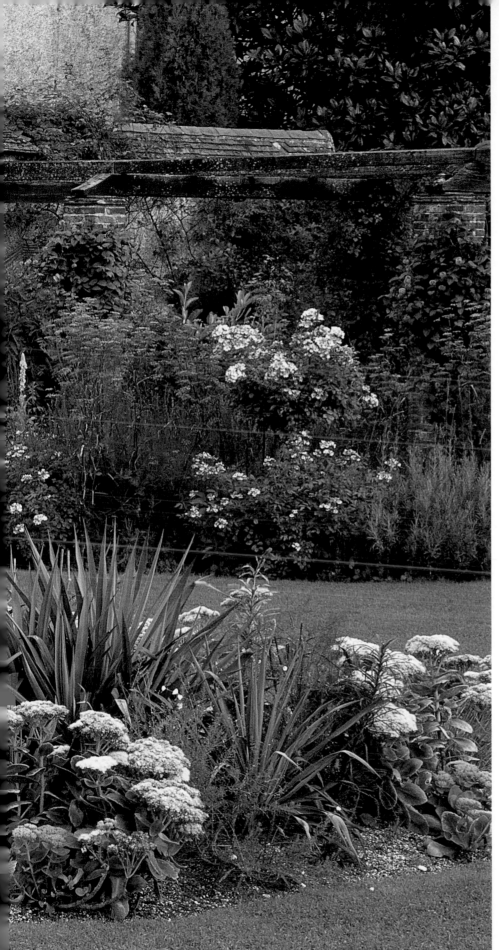

LEFT *At the Bois des Moutiers, in Normandy, France, an autumn garden huddles around a sundial. The house was built during the Arts and Crafts period in the early 1900s by the English architect Edwin Lutyens. Sundial gardens were a favorite motif of his (he often designed the hardscape as well) and of gardeners generally during this time. Sundials hark back to the historic gardens of Tudor England and Renaissance Italy, which were the model for so many Arts and Crafts garden designers and were the focal point of hedge-enclosed garden rooms. The inscriptions were usually melancholic, referring to the transience of life and the gardener's mortality: "Thou seest the hour, but knowest not the hour." In autumn, the garden's life cycle comes full circle, so what could be more appropriate?*

Boxwood can vary in leaf color and size, and yew raised from seed can be extremely variable and would give an uneven appearance to what is meant to be a uniform feature.

Lollipop or mop-head standards are popular for container-grown topiary and can often be purchased ready-shaped. Rosemary, sweet bay, scented-leaf geraniums, patio roses, and lemon verbena as well as common boxwood (*Buxus sempervirens*) are often seen as the central feature in urns and other formal containers. Often these plants will only survive if brought indoors during winter. Indeed, in cold climates, the key to success with half-hardy shrubs like lemon verbena and scented-leaf geraniums is to overwinter them in a frostfree place and stop watering until early spring, when they should be encouraged out of dormancy and pruned of the previous year's growth.

MAKE MINE A MICROCLIMATE

One last word about the importance of hedges and screens in the garden—in autumn or otherwise—is that careful positioning can help you garden by creating microclimates

LEFT *A rustic gazebo made of hazel wands stands out in its nakedness in an early autumn border, but by the end of the season as the garden loses its color and the trees their foliage, it will blend in unnoticably.*

RIGHT *A beautifully observed sculpture of a soaring red kite, a rare Welsh bird of prey, graces the autumnal garden, reminding us that the seasons fly by on silent wings.*

within the overall garden. Just as the old field hedge protected my English garden in rural Norfolk from the prevailing southwest wind, so the hornbeam hedge sheltered the perennial border in front of it from the freezing fogs and gales that blew in off the North Sea, straight from the Ural Mountains. So for most Norfolk gardens and other gardens where wind is a major feature, establishing shelter-belt protection is of prime importance. And within the garden hedges can be used to further increase zones of relative stillness.

You can also exploit the natural microclimates that occur in your garden. In cold climates, notice where the early morning sun first strikes; this will be the first spot to warm and not a good place to put plants that flower early, since the quick thaw would damage delicate plant tissues. Put them instead on a southwest-facing aspect so that they

ABOVE *Boldly planted containers using tender exotics are at their best in autumn. The centerpiece of this urn is a century plant.*

warm up gently. Early summer-flowering plants can often be ruined by a snap late frost, so put them against a cooler northwest-facing aspect so that flowering is held back until the frosts are truly over. A thick blanket of mulch laid in the autumn over early flowering perennials or bulbs also helps to keep them tucked up underground until the danger of frost damage is over.

Color can affect the relative warmth in a garden. In vegetable gardens, a black plastic covering warms up the soil more quickly than a clear plastic one. Similarly, the effect of burning a prairie is to leave behind a deposit of black stubble, which then warms more rapidly, helping prairie plant seeds to germinate. Hard-landscaping materials can have the same effect. A brick wall stores heat, which is why fruit trees are often trained against them. Paving stones too can store heat that radiates into the surrounding soil to help marginal rock plants through a frosty weather.

Understand the lay of the land. A frost pocket will form at the lowest point on sloping ground because cold air flows downhill; even the bottom of a south-facing slope will be the last place in the garden to warm up, while the top of the slope will warm quickly. Think about where you are naturalizing those narcissi and early spring bulbs!

In warm climates, the trick is to provide pockets of cool shade, so dividing a wide-open sunny space—like my new garden—with a series of low hedges or a vine-covered trellis will enlarge the plant palette. I'm even thinking about putting topiary to work, and "cloud-pruning" an evergreen shrub to shade our air conditioning unit, which unfortunately is located against a southwest-facing wall.

POTS AND PATHS

Container gardens are for those of us without a "grounded" garden, like my friend Lee, whose garden is on the rooftop of his four-floor building in downtown Manhattan. It is his pride and joy, and since he's an interior designer it gives him the opportunity to take his talent outdoors. Lee observes the changing seasons by tending his carefully amassed collection of very large, very simple containers, all of which are painted black. Some of these are permanently planted with silver-leaved shrubs and deciduous trees, including a white-barked birch. Along the low parapet wall he has trained a white-flowered wisteria; all the perennials have white flowers and the seasonal bulbs and annuals are also white. In the summer, when foliage and flower are in full fettle, the dark containers disappear and the impression is of a cool leafy glade, only two blocks from Macy's on 7th Avenue. By October, Lee is beginning the winterizing process; clearing the perennial "beds" of faded top growth, removing wilted summer bedding, and adding a few more bulbs for spring color beneath the trees. Some pots are brought indoors, others are heavily mulched with straw.

In England, during early autumn I would bring the standard lemon verbenas into the greenhouse along with the scented-leaf geraniums and collection of succulent plants that spent the fine weather of spring and summer on a sunny, south-facing step. I generally tried to tidy these up, (except for the verbena, which kept its old growth until spring), by removing dead stems and faded leaves. Any plants that had outgrown their containers were repotted, so that in spring new growth was not checked by their being disturbed. Many of the most useful container plants are half-hardy, such as the highly colorful coleus, gazania, sweet potato vine (*Ipomoea batatas*), Swedish ivy, giant hyssop, cardoon, pineapple flower, and New Zealand flax. They are "useful" because they continue putting on a fine show right up to first frosts. They can be increased by taking cuttings in late summer into early autumn or by making divisions or potting offsets.

Autumn is the time for maintenance work on containers. Too often we forget that the fabric of the garden requires attention if it is to play its supporting role in the unfolding drama of the seasons. As you repot container plants, inspect the old pots for cracks and dings. Unless they are priceless urns, it is really not worth keeping them, better to bust them up and use the shards to provide adequate drainage in the bottom of new containers. Those you keep should be brushed out and then washed in a solution of warm water and household disinfectant to clean off algae. Plastic containers can become brittle over time and with exposure to sunlight, so assess the durability of any you are using. Wood half-barrels will eventually rot and so offer an invitation to insect pests. Are there any ant colonies establishing themselves in containers of ornamental shrubs? Their tunneling exposes the roots to more air than they require and will eventually kill the plant, so get the ants first by watering in an ant-specific pesticide.

In his book *Garden Paths*, Vermont-based garden designer Gordon Hayward clearly sets out the design and construction of what is ultimately the most important landscape feature: "The path . . . is far more than a means of getting from here to there on dry, solid ground. It is a way to organize your thinking about garden design: it is a way to organize space and clarify the meaning of your whole garden . . . It invites, even pulls people into the garden.

have been worn bald or thin in places or the material may be "leaking" from the edges into the flower beds. Rake it over and spread new mulch to keep up the levels. Brick and concrete paths that pass through shady parts of the garden can become slippery with moss and algae, so wash them down with a good stiff brush and a demossing solution. Similarly, wood decks and duckboards will not last forever, so check them for damage.

If paths are the main arteries of the garden, then the potting shed is the nerve center, and autumn is a good time to clear out the previous year's old seed packets, broken pots, squashed seed trays, tangled twine, and cobwebs, so that come spring the synapses will be snapping freely as you get to work. Clean all pots and seed trays with disinfectant and stack them neatly according to size. Sort through plant labels; the white plastic ones can be cleaned of old names by scrubbing lightly with an abrasive kitchen cleanser.

Check over all garden tools and clean off dirt that has encrusted around the handles. Oil and grease the moving parts and blades of cutting tools, and take the lawn mower to be serviced once you have given the grass its final cut of the year. Bring the hose indoors rather than leaving it to rot in the elements, and check over the irrigation system in the kitchen garden (if you have such a system). Clean and empty water barrels. Just as we give the house a spring cleaning, we can give the garden its autumn cleaning. It helps to make your winter hibernation much more relaxed knowing that, for a while at least, as you enjoy other favorite pastimes, it is possible not to feel the pressure of garden work waiting.

To look at a garden in terms of its paths, then is to look at the garden as whole, for it is the path that links all parts and thus helps create a sense of place."

Take the time in autumn to clear the path (especially brick or stone-paved paths) of weeds at the same time as you are weeding the flower beds. If the path is made of bark or wood mulch, pine needles, or other organic material, it may

During the off-season, I have always particularly enjoyed browsing through old gardening books, seeking inspiration or just generally musing on how very little things really do change over the centuries. One of my favorites is *Pot Pourri from a Surrey Garden*, written by Mrs. C. W. Earle, a contemporary (and some say rival) of Gertrude Jekyll. She is solidly down-to-earth with her comments and advice. Picking up her volume now, as autumn plays around my heels, I read the following in the chapter devoted to September: "In spite of all the charming things Mr. [William] Robinson says about it, 'wild gardening' is, I am sure, a delusion and a snare . . . it requires endless care, and is always extending in all directions in search of fresh soil. What is possible is to have the appearance of a wild garden in consequence of the most *judicious planting, with consummate knowledge and experience of the plants that will do well in the soil if they are just a little assisted at the time of planting.*" (My italics.)

She notices, too, the tameness of the robins as we dig the garden, the dewy gossamer that hangs in the garden and the way the flowers shine out of the early mists as the low-angled autumn light strikes across the garden. She recalls, too, the remark of a friend whose garden is on England's east coast, maybe in Norfolk, for the comment is about how the wind will always scatter the autumn leaves before they have a chance to touch the ground. Feeling rather like those windblown leaves, I wonder, as I contemplate the future as a gardener in Texas, whether the memory of my English autumn garden will ever fade? I doubt it.

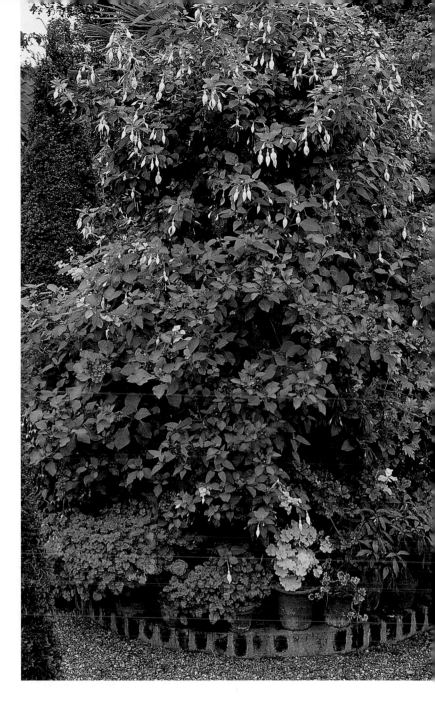

LEFT & ABOVE *Each year at the Old Vicarage, Alan Gray makes masterful container displays using a wide range of fuchsias, solanums, geraniums, pineapple flower, honey bush, and countless other exotics chosen for the vibrancy of their shape and color. The fuchsia tower, right, is an assortment of bicolor pelargonium and scented geraniums, huddled around a huge urn planted with standard and trailing fuchsias. If you are going to container garden, be bold about it!*

GREAT AUTUMN PLANTS

There are all sorts of reasons to select a plant for the garden: good foliage texture, an exciting perfume, an unusual shape, an architectural form, outstanding color. When it comes to choosing a great autumn plant, however, color is the single most relevant characteristic. In autumn, if the flowers are especially vivid, the berries bright, or the foliage adds a subtle range of hues to the fading fabric of the garden scheme, the plant gets noticed.

As I described in *Leaf, Bark and Berry,* plants in the natural landscape are displayed in layers: tree canopy above shrub and perennial layer, beneath which shelter the annuals, biennials, small bulbs, and groundcover. Manipulate this face of nature in mixed border plantings or in William Robinson–style "wild gardens," mindful all the while of suiting plants to the site and each other, is how we create gardens. I hope that the plants described in the following pages will help you to add layers of color to your garden in autumn, so that the passage of summer to winter turns likes the pages of a fascinating novel.

FOLIAGE

The layered planting of trees and shrubs comes vividly to life in autumn, composed as it is of a wide variety of differently sized and shaped plants that display their best color just before leaf fall. Beneath the mottled gray trunk of a tall-growing eucalyptus (previous page), smaller, bright-leafed trees like kousa dogwood, *Cornus kousa*, and paperbark maple, *Acer griseum*, cast their foliage over equally warm-hued medium-size shrubs like wine-red barberry. Ornamental grasses and low-growing shrubs including Japanese spiraea, *Spiraea japonica*, and gray-leafed *Brachyglottis greyi*, occupy the bottom layer of this mixed grouping. All these plants have a preference for moisture-retentive soil and slightly acid conditions, as well as having something else to offer, such as the dogwood's papery white bracts in spring, or the maple's year-long display of the cinnamon-red peeling bark (previous page inset).

Acers hold the most reward for autumn gardenmaking; there is a huge number of maples to choose from, some with fabulous color or remarkable bark, or both. The intensity of the color will vary with the region, being softer in mild climates.

Among the large growing species, the silver maple, *A. saccharinum* (named for the silvery sheen of the underside of the leaves), and the common sycamore, *A. pseudoplatanus,* have little to recommend them other than quick growth—and the sycamore will self-sow anywhere and everywhere. The sugar maple, *A. saccharum*, is The Tree of New England fall-color scenes. It is robustly hardy and grows to at least 120 feet, so needs

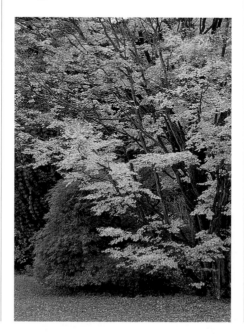

space to show to its best. In smaller gardens and for purely ornamental purposes, the Japanese maples, cultivars of *A. palmatum*, are the ones to choose. These include small trees, some growing to about 30 feet tall, with nicely shaped spreading crowns, as well as shrub-size or dwarf trees that form mounds of lacy foliage. These are the sort most frequently used as accent plants or among perennials in a mixed border. *A. palmatum* 'Dissectum Atropurpureum' (above) is unquestionably the best known and widely used for its finely divided dentate leaves that take on a deepening purple tone as the seasons progress. 'Osakazuki' is a stalwart in the group, with flame red autumn foliage. The cultivar 'Senkaki', properly known as 'Sango-kaku', has good yellow-colored leaves that accentuate the coral-tinted bark. It is seen at left with the russet red 'Dissectum' and above, grown as small grove. Young trees have the most deeply colored bark, but mature trees have an elegant shape with a broad, spreading crown.

Some of the Japanese maples are desirable for their oddly shaped leaves; 'Okushimo' has a stiff upright habit and its lobed leaves that resemble the splayed toes of a bird's foot. Among palmatums, 'Orido-nishiki' has the pret-

tiest variegation, with shades of pink, green, white and cream changing through the seasons. 'Karasugawa' is almost entirely pink in leaf and stem, and the new growth is white stained with a rosy glow. It is not robust and requires shade and shelter, so is best suited to container growing.

Many of the other small-growing cultivars among the palmatum group are ideal for container growing. Use a potting mix that will hold moisture well (containers quickly become arid zones!) and use a slow-release fertilizer to keep up levels of available nutrients. Where winter

temperatures drop below freezing, it is advisable to either bring container grown plants under cover or to insulate the containers by covering them in bubble wrap and burlap sacking.

Well-drained sandy loam, on the acid side of neutral, suits Japanese maples best. They are not deep rooting, so mulching, especially in hot climates, will help to keep the roots moist in summer. In mild climates they do well in sun, although strong sun will scorch the leaves, so position them where they will receive shade during the hottest part of the day.

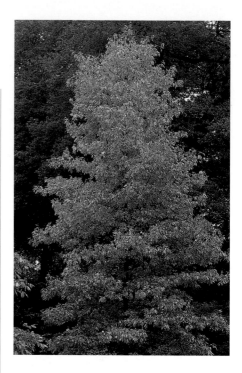

Amelanchier canadensis (above), the serviceberry of North America and the snowy mespilus of Europe, deserves both common names for the good service it does in the garden all year round and the tiny white flowers of early spring. Held in loose clusters amid the ruddy brown-tinted foliage, the flowers look like late-falling snow, but by the beginning of autumn, the foliage is turning a vibrant flaming red-orange and the flowers have turned to berries that ripen from pale yellow to deep purple. Other species are equally attractive; *A. lamarckii* has silky juvenile foliage, the largest flower clusters, and the most stunning autumn color among the species. Native to the Allegheny mountains, this species is fairly hardy and does best in neutral to acid soil in sun or part shade. They are suckering shrubs that can be grown as small, multibranched trees. They have a delicate gracefulness, and are ideally suited to small gardens.

Ampelopsis brevipedunculata 'Elegans' (below) is less vigorous than some vines, only growing to about 10 feet. With its heavy mottling of cream and pink variegation, this tendril climber needs a shady spot to prevent scorching and in cold-zone gardens some protection against freezing. It can be used to clothe a low retaining wall or as groundcover among shrubs and small trees that will provide the necessary shade and shelter. Use among dark evergreens to provide a showcase background. The little specks of white are the juvenile fruit, which mature to dark blue, adding another color to the display. Any soil is suitable, as long as it is moisture retentive.

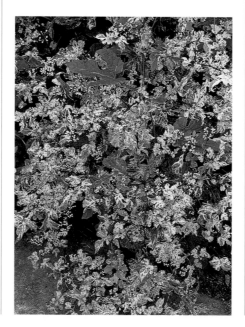

Carya glabra (above) is commonly known as the pignut or pignut hickory. It makes a tall-growing tree to 80 feet with a prettily shaped conical crown in its early years. It has compound leaves of five lobes rather like those of its relative the walnut; they turn to a fresh butter yellow in autumn. The pignut is more commonly seen in the eastern United States than in the United Kingdom, but makes a fine specimen tree in either location. Since the tree resents being transplanted you might want to grow a pignut from seed. It needs rich, loamy soil. *C. ovata*, the shagbark hickory, has good autumn color and distinctive rough, peeling bark.

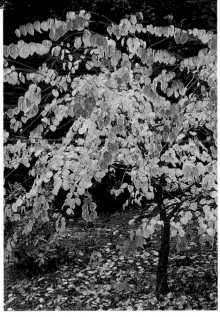

Cercidiphyllum japonicum (above and below right) is the treasured Katsura tree of Japanese gardens. It has a graceful, tiered pagodalike outline and shimmering bright yellow autumn foliage that will illuminate the garden on a dull day as surely as a 100-watt bulb! All this visual stimulus is augmented by an olfactory one: The fallen leaves spread out in a golden pool beneath the naked boughs and give off the scent of melted chocolate. The finest example I know is at the entrance to the Japanese tea garden in the Blodell Reserve on Bainbridge Island in Puget Sound. Even when leafless in the naked depth of winter, the tree has a shapely presence. A shrubby relative of the Katsura, *Disanthus cercidifolius* has redder

tints and smaller leaves and is quite rare in cultivation. Both hate lime and need deep, moist, acid soil to do their best.

Cercis canadensis 'Forest Pansy' (above), an especially well-colored cultivar of the eastern redbud, is much loved by gardeners in the United States from the mountains of Virginia to the Hill Country of Texas. In the United Kingdom and Southern Europe, its counterpart is the Judas tree, *C. siliquastrum*, which William Robinson remarked as having been grown in English gardens for nearly 300 years. Both species have rosy-pink flowers on naked branches in the spring and good autumn color. They are well-suited to growing in alkaline soils but will also tolerate acid conditions. They will eventually grow to 30 to 40 feet, becoming broad-crowned trees with spreading branches. As Robinson pointed out, it is the young trees that flower most profusely.

Enkianthus campanulatus (above) is the best of the large to medium-size shrubs in this genus. The branches are held in loose tiers from which hang pendulous clusters of tiny, pink-tinted white bell-shaped flowers in early summer. The leaves cluster in whorls around the branches, emphasizing the tiered outline of the shrub. But it is the rich purpling of the foliage in autumn, enhanced by shades of yellow, red, and orange, that really makes this shrub outstanding. This species usually grows to roughly 12 feet, although in ideal conditions of moist, acid soil in a woodland setting, it can grow to be much taller. *E. perulatus* is about half the size of its sister, but with the same pendent flower clusters and excellent autumn color. It, too, requires moist, acid soil.

E. cernuus f. *rubens* (above) is a red-flowered form of the species that grows to a height midway between two others.

Euonymus alatus, the winged spindle tree, holds its spreading branches like the ribs of a fan decked out in warm red foliage and hung with dainty clusters of ruby-red fruit. Each berry is shaped like a winged lantern and splits open to reveal the fleshy coral fruit inside. It's an easy-to-grow shrub for any soil and in sun or part shade. The species has "winged" bark, vertical striations that stand away from the surface, giving this deciduous shrub a good texture during winter. The variety *E. a.* var. *apterus* (above), does not have this feature.

Fothergilla major (above) lights up the space beneath the dark branches of *Acer palmatum* 'Osakazuki', demonstrating the dynamic effects that can be established with layered planting. Throughout the summer the fothergilla is a rather dull plant, its leaves a dusty gray-green. But it compensates by producing scented white bottle-brush flowers on naked stems in spring, while in autumn the leaves are transformed to shades of red, purple, orange, and yellow.

Fothergilla species require neutral to acid soils, partial shade, and moisture-retentive soil, and so they like to grow in woodland settings or beneath small trees in a garden. *F. major* grows to about 6 feet—but very slowly. *F. gardenii* only reaches about 4 feet and has a mounded habit. The foliage of *F. g.* 'Blue Mist' is prettily tinted a steely blue.

This genus, commonly named witch alder, is part of the Hamamelidaceae family and is related to witch hazel.

Hamamelis mollis (below), Chinese witch hazel, also bears softly scented flowers in early spring. They resemble little shreds of orange or lemon peel stuck in tight clusters along the naked branches. These large shrubs or small trees grow slowly. However, it's worth the wait. A mature plant can be 15 to 20 feet tall with a broad spreading crown and carries its perfumed flowers well above companion plants, casting a vivid golden autumn spell over the garden. Other witch hazels—all with good autumn coloring—include the cultivars of *H. × intermedia* with flowers variously colored coppery orange ('Jelena'), pale butter-cream yellow ('Pallida') and red ('Ruby Glow') and the cultivar *H. vernalis* 'Sandra', which has purple-flushed young foliage that turns to the best of autumn golds and red. This last plant grows to 10 feet, and has a tendency to sucker. Witch hazels prefer partial shade and neutral to acid soil that is moisture retentive.

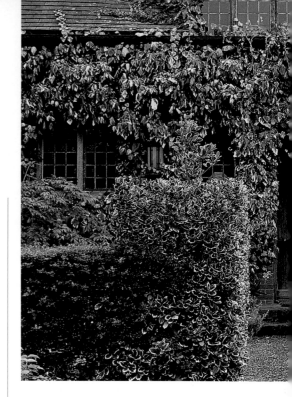

through a shady woodland makes a spectacular show, and even two or three plants add a gentle grace to a mixed group. It will grow in any soil, including chalk.

H. quercifolia (below) is the oakleaf hydrangea, so called for the shape of its leaves, which color well in autumn in shades of purple and russet red on peeling cinnamon-bark stems. These rich tints perfectly complement the white flowerheads, which are similar in shape to those of *H. paniculata* but rounder. The plant has a sprawling, "picturesque" habit. Grow it in rich, moisture-retentive soil in partial shade. It is not entirely hardy, and does its very best in warm gardens, so give it shelter.

Hydrangea paniculata (above) can be distinguished from the widely popular mop-head and lace-cap hydrangeas by its plumelike flowerheads. These are conical in shape, like out-of-season lilacs colored white to blushing pink, and appear at the tip of every branch. This hydrangea is widely grown in Japanese gardens. An extremely hardy plant, it will tolerate even quite warm climates. It can become tall and leggy, but pruning back hard in early spring will control its straggliness and encourage plenty of new growth to provide the late-summer flowers—which only appear on the new season's growth. It will grow in sun or partial shade; an avenue lined with this species, weaving

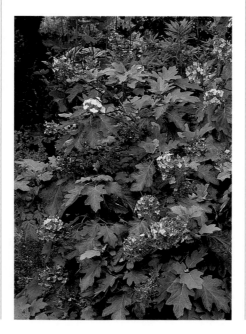

Ilex (above) is one of the most useful shrubs a gardener can grow; as William Robinson wrote, "As regards the uses of the Holly, they are so many in the garden that it is difficult even to generalize them. As shelter in bold groups, dividing lines, hedges, beautiful effects of fruit in autumn, masses of evergreen foliage, bright glistening color from variegated kinds . . . every kind of delightful use may be found for them in gardens."

The light-reflecting quality of its glossy evergreen leaves is part of holly's great charm, adding depth to a mixed group of deciduous and evergreen shrubs. The berries also bring color to the autumn garden and range in color, depending on the species, from bright yellow to ruby red. There is also a daunting selection of leaf shapes, texture, variegation, and color to choose from. Among the most popular variegated sorts of the common English holly, *I. aquifolium*, are 'Argentea Marginata',

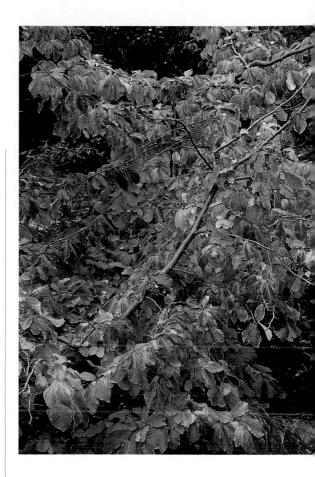

'Silver Queen', and 'Handsworth New Silver', all with white variegation; 'Golden Milkboy' and 'Golden Queen' have yellow variegation. *I. a.* 'Green Pillar' is solidly green and sturdily erect, while 'Myrtifolia' has small green leaves. 'Ferox' is the hedgehog holly, so called for the spine-covered surface of the leaves. Some hollies have a distinct blue cast to the leaves, especially *I. × meserveae* 'Blue Angel', 'Blue Prince', and 'Blue Princess'.

I. × altaclerensis is a natural, tall-growing, robust garden hybrid that has a pleasing pyramidal shape; most are nearly thornless. These are tall-growing and robust in appearance. One of the most popular cultivars is 'Lawsoniana', which has bold yellow splashes on the leaves. *I. × a* 'Golden King' is also widely grown, and despite its name, is a female plant. Sex is important to note when making a selection, since to have berries it is essential to grow both male and female plants.

Nyssa sylvatica (below) is the tupelo tree of the eastern and southern United States. It is fairly hardy and will grow in any moist ground quite happily and up to 100 feet tall—it really needs plenty of room to show off its elegant pyramidal shape. The young foliage is bright green, and throughout summer it holds a glossy gleam, turning in autumn to all the shades of a harvest sunset. Next to the sweetgum, this is one of the best specimen trees for a fall garden. It is best suited to acid soils.

Parrotia persica (above), the Persian ironwood, is another splendid specimen for the autumn garden. It has an elegant habit, growing slowly to make a medium-size tree of about 30 feet in height, usually with several trunks supporting a broad, horizontally spreading crown. The foliage is a dull green color in summer, but during autumn the downward curving leaves turn from yellow through dark red to purple. This tree does well on moisture-retentive, neutral to chalky soils, in sun or partial shade position. It is a relative of the witch hazel.

Parthenocissus tricuspidata (left) is the variously hated or loved Boston ivy. It is said to destroy walls by its habit of climbing, using little suckering rootlets to attach itself to the mortar (others claim that the leaves protect the brickwork from the elements). It is loved for the brightness of its autumn color, and there is no question that it and its relative, the five-lobed *P. quinquefolia* (Virginia creeper), epitomize autumn coloring. But both should be used sparingly. Gertrude Jekyll made the valid point that climbers should not be allowed to completely disguise the architecture that supports them (unless, of course, that was the whole point of planting them in the first place). *Parthenocissus* will grow anywhere if the soil is well drained.

Polystichum setiferum (above) is a common woodland fern in both northern Europe and North America, where it grows easily in the light cool shade and moist, humus-rich soil of the forest floor and woodland edge. There are many other species and some cultivars that have distinctly curious leaf formations, like 'Densum' which I can only describe as having leaves that are fully double; it looks like an especially fluffy plume of feathers. When they are young, the habit of most of these ferns makes them resemble shuttlecocks, and the upright-growing fronds look exceptionally pretty waving over bright-colored groundcover or beneath the shade of an autumn-tinted shrub, like the red-tinted leaves of *Viburnum plicatum,* shown here.

Prunus species and cultivars are many and all have something worth writing about, but for autumn color the ornamental cherry species, *P. sargentii* (above), remains my favorite. A young tree planted in moist but well-drained soil in sun or part shade, will quickly make a medium-size tree up to 25 feet tall. The tree has an upward-spreading outline, like a funnel or martini glass, and the pendulous clusters of pale pinky white flowers appear in early spring, followed closely by the copper-tinted juvenile leaves—very elegant. In autumn the leaves cling, and in my garden, at least, seemed to change overnight from green to flaming tones of yellow, red, and orange. Then they

seemed to drop just as suddenly, making a pool of sunbeams on the dewy autumn grass. All this theater makes this one tree that I do not hesitate to recommend for the small garden.

P. serrula (above) is another cherry worth having, but for its bark rather than its visual bite. The sheen and warm glow of the peeling rust-red bark is this tree's main claim to garden space, although it does have a pretty spreading habit and pleasing white flowers in spring. The bark is good all year round, so call this another winner.

P. 'Mount Fuji' (above) is typical of many of the ornamental cherries in having good autumn color. It, too, is a medium-size tree, and the spring flower show is composed of quite large, single white blossoms in pendent clusters. But the best for single flowers and with good autumn color is the great white cherry, *P.* 'Taihaku'.

Quercus rubra (left), or red oak, along with the sugar maple, is one of the main players in the New England autumn color cast. Similarly, it lights up many an English landscape but perhaps without the vivacity it displays in America. In Texas, too, the red oak is a favorite autumn tree, and its bright red thumbprint can be easily spotted among the dull-green crowns of the evergreen live oaks (*Q. virginiana*) that cloak the Hill Country.

Oaks grow slowly into large statuesque trees (this is what makes their wood so dense and valuable), and will grow in most soils in sun or part shade. *Q. coccinea*, the scarlet oak, moreover, is a relatively fast-growing, medium-sized tree and has good red coloring—some would say the best of all.

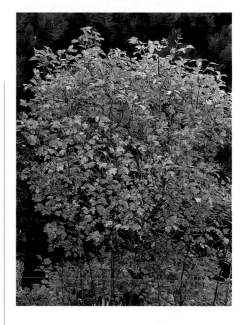

Rhus typhina (above), the staghorn sumac, makes a spectacular display in autumn with its brilliant red, compound leaves gracefully displayed on spreading branches. Each leaflet of the cultivar *R. t.* 'Dissecta' is deeply toothed, giving this shrub a much lacier appearance with the same flaming color. This shrub takes its common name from the fuzzy texture of the new shoots in spring, which recall the down on the antlers of a young stag. The flowers, too (right), are enjoyed for their curious velvety texture. Sumac is a relative of the other brilliant autumn showoff *Cotinus coggygria*, or smoke tree, with its self-descriptively named cultivars such as 'Royal Purple', 'Pink Champagne', and 'Flame'.

These colorful shrubs will grow in any soil in sun or part shade. Sumac has a tendency to sucker, but it is easily controlled by pulling out young upstarts.

Viburnum sargentii (above) displays its bright red, glossy berries against soft gold foliage; *V. s.* 'Onondaga' is even more dramatically colored. The cultivar has a more upright habit than the species, and the young foliage is colored soft purple-green in spring and deepens to a dusky maroon in autumn. The flower umbels are small and white, shining out from amid the dark leaves. This is a good plant for a somber corner in shade and moisture-retentive soil.

Vitis is the grape genus, which includes some very autumnally attractive species, as well as the delicious sorts used for making wine. For breathtaking foliage, size-wise, and color-wise, *V. coignetiae* (above and right), is hard to beat. Above, it is happily mixed with *Clematis orientalis*, whose wispy seedheads provide an interesting textural contrast with the vine's large leaves. *V. coignetiae* is a hardy, rampant grower, once established, and can be cut down to the knuckle each spring, or back to a trained framework of main branches, from where it will throw long wands that are soon covered in huge, heart-shaped leaves. These are deeply veined and rough in texture, and in the autumn turn the best shades of red and purple. But it really needs room to spread—in my English garden it consumed the garage, but then I never was much on judicious pruning, preferring to let things romp. I've also grown *V. vinifera* 'Purpurea', with its dark purple leaves and fruit, and *V.* 'Brant', another decorative variety, which is mentioned in chapter 4, The Lasting Framework. Of all the grape vines in cultivation, to date these three are the only ones that have been given the Award of Garden Merit by the Royal Horticultural Society. Well-drained soil in a sunny position suits them best.

GRASSES

Once underappreciated, ornamental grasses, bamboos, and forbs in general are enjoying a newfound stardom. From Munich to Seattle the graceful blades and twitching seedheads are very much in vogue as the main ingredient in "natural," "wild," "ecological," and "new perennial" gardens—call them what you will. This makes sense, of course, when you observe that much of nature's planting is woven into a grass matrix.

Cortaderia selloana 'Sunningdale Silver' (previous page) is one of the most widely grown of those South American natives— the fabulous pampas grasses. The cultivar and the species, *C. selloana* (above left), have towering, ultrafluffy plumes, but there are smaller growing varieties, such as *C. s.* 'Pumila', which is good in small gardens, and the gold-variegated *C. s.* 'Aureolineata' with yellow stripes running down each leaf blade.

Forming huge clumps, pampas grass begins to flower in late summer carrying the erect stems—up to 9 feet tall— throughout the autumn and winter. By the end of the season, the plumes look pretty shabby and so should be cut down.

Plant in the spring in deep, sandy, well-drained soil in a sheltered spot out of cold winds for the best results.

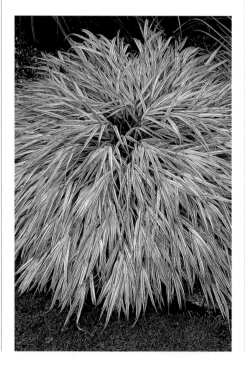

Hordeum jubatum (above), the squirreltail barley or squirreltail grass, is a short-lived perennial that is most generally grown as an annual. It is usually cultivated for its fine seedheads, which dry well for decorations, and less often simply because it is such a good mingler in the garden. It does best in dry soil—too much moisture makes it "fat" and the plumes are less likely to survive cutting and drying well.

Hakonechloa macra 'Aureola' (below left) is a grass much used in Japanese gardens, probably because of its waterfall-like spray of golden variegated foliage that moves languorously when stirred by the breeze. It does best in a sheltered, partly shaded site, although in cool climates it can be put in the sun where it will color nicely with a reddish blush.

Miscanthus, or eulalia grass, is in my estimation the grass genus *par excellence*. The foliage is varied and refined, the flower plumes delicately tinted with a silken sheen. The flowers appear late in the summer and carry on well through autumn and winter. There is also a good selection of size and height from which to choose.

Don't cram the plants into borders; give them space to breathe so that their graceful form is displayed without hindrance—*Miscanthus* is definitely an 'architectural' plant.

M. sinensis is the species most often grown in gardens and there are numerous cultivars ranging in height from 4 feet (*M. s.* 'Kleine Silberspinne') to 7 feet (*M. s.* 'Grosse Fontäne'). *M. s.* 'Zebrinus' (above) is a popular variety that is notable for the yellow variegation that runs across each leaf blade, while *M. s.* 'Malepartus' (left), has the most pronounced red autumn coloring of the genus.

The feathery plumes of all *Miscanthus* are a good feature, and they have a strong visual and tactile quality thanks to their clump-forming grasses in conjunction with other forbs and perennials. In this small section of Mark Brown's *Miscanthus* border he has used (from foreground to back), the grass *Deschampsia cespitosa* 'Goldtau', white-flowered *Sedum spectabile* 'Stardust', *M. sinensis* 'Ferne Osten', the common herb fennel (*Foeniculum vulgare*), *M. s.* 'Rotsilber' and *M. s.* 'Ernst Pagels'. Incidentally, *Deschampsia*, or tufted hair grass, is another gorgeous autumn-flowering grass, with long loose flower panicles of extreme delicacy that dry from soft wine red to bright biscuit brown. In contrast, the leaves are long, spiky in texture and dark glossy green. It will seed freely.

soft glossy texture, which catches the sunlight and the eye. *M.* 'Silberfeder' (above), which translates as "Silver Feather," earned its name for just these reasons.

Miscanthus will grow in most soils, but really does its best in deeply dug, humus-rich soil that is well drained but not dry. The spent flower spikes and foliage can be cut down to a height of 10 to 12 inches in the spring; then mulch the plants with well-rotted compost. Plants can also be lifted, divided, and replanted in the spring.

A mixed border of *Miscanthus* (right), shows what can be done with these

Molinia caerulea 'Variegata' (above) is the variegated form of moor grass, a clumping purple perennial that is native to acid heathland. This form is the one most often found in gardens, thanks to the white stripe that runs the length of each leaf, accentuating the graceful curve and movement of the foliage. The erect flower stems turn burnished gold in autumn and stand well above the leaves. Its relative, *M. c.* ssp. *arundinacea* is another bundle of golden autumn color, with stiff flower stems and tidy clumping foliage. These grasses are generally small growing, typically only 3 to 4 feet, and are ideal for heavy, acid, moisture-retentive soil.

Stipa is the genus that provides the other "must grow" grasses, and I have tried the three shown here and will happily do so again. Nothing quite captures the eye like *S. gigantea* (above), with its golden seed spikes waving in the breeze above the delicately leaved tussocks of dusky green foliage. It's a sight to make you stand still and contemplate—something one should find frequent occasion to do in a garden. From flower tip to leaf base, this grass is about 6 feet tall. Don't crowd it; use it as a signpost plant or to give particular emphasis to a specific garden area, and

make sure the sunlight can catch the seedheads in autumn. Its only weakness is that the stems are quite pliant, and a stiff breeze can knock them to the ground and end the show, so select a sheltered but sunny corner.

Similarly, but on a less grand scale, *S. tenuissima* (right), Mexican feather grass, has stunning seedheads like trailing threads of spun silver. Here they are spilling over the frosted gray-green foliage rosettes of *Phlomis samia*. This is the sort of contrast that is attainable with ornamental grasses; playing broad leaf against narrow leaf to create varied textures and shadow. I have found that this particular *Stipa* grows easily from seed; simply pull the threads from the seedheads and lay them in a tray of moist compost. Cover them with a sifting of soil, or spread them thinly in a prepared seedbed and cover lightly. Keep well watered until germination, and there will soon be lots of little bright green shaving brushes ready to plant out in the garden. This grass works especially well with members of the Compositae family like *Anthemis*.

Stipa calamagrostis (above) is one of the most free-flowering of all the grasses, with the fluffy plumes appearing in midsummer and carrying right through autumn and winter. It is so dependable, it can almost be boring, except for its grace and winning ways as a flower for drying. Massed plantings of this *Stipa*, as seen here with *Sedum* 'Strawberries and Cream', are most effective. One other *Stipa* to be sure to grow is *S. arundinacea* because of its graceful waterfall of foliage that takes on a rusty orange glow in autumn.

All that these grasses require is a sunny spot and well-drained soil that doesn't dry out completely. I don't recommend ever cutting them down. Rake through the foliage with your fingers during the early spring to remove the spent flowerheads and any dead foliage.

BERRIES

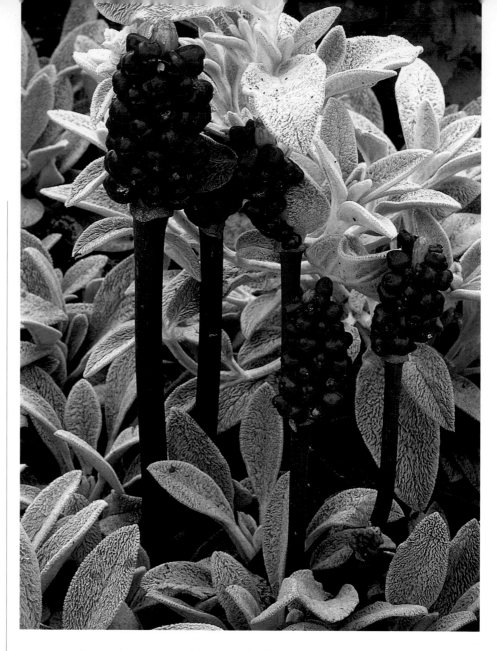

Summer flowers give way to seed-bearing, autumn fruit as part of the regenerative process of nature. Gardens benefit from this with the ornamental riches of many varieties of brightly colored, curiously formed, glistening, or differently textured berries and seed-containing pods.

Berries are *indehiscent*, which means that they do not open to disperse their cache of seed, as a *dehiscent* pod would do. A berry, instead, contains the seed in a protective shell. The seed is not dispersed until the shell rots away or is digested by an animal; berry-eating birds are among the best seed-scatterers in nature.

Some dehiscent plants have especially attractive pods or bracts, like *Amicia zygomeris* (previous page), a member of the pea family, Leguminosae, from the woodlands of western Mexico. The butterflylike purple-stained wings at the leaf axils make this a most unusual autumn ornamental. The top growth will not withstand frost, but it will shoot again from the roots if protected by mulch.

Arum maculatum, known as cuckoopint and lords-and-ladies, is a hedgerow plant. Its large spade-shaped leaves appear in spring and are followed by an erect, hooded flower spathe that gives way to a spike of orange to crimson berries, similar to the spike of *A. italicum* ssp. *albispathum* 'Marmoratum' (above). The flare of red against the soft gray leaves of *Stachys byzantina* 'Cotton Boll' (known as wooly betony or lamb's-ears) is as fine an autumn feature as you could care to have. Earlier in the year, the silvery veins of the arum's foliage blend well with the gray of the lamb's-ears. Arums generally prefer deep moist soil, but I have grown just this combination in free-draining, sandy soil and really enjoyed the seasonal show.

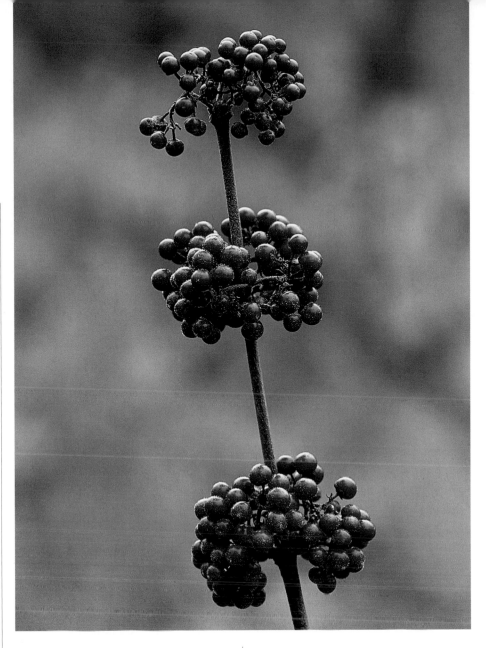

Berberis (barberry) is a large genus of ever-green, semievergreen, and deciduous shrubs that are extremely popular for their pretty flower clusters. Some also have attractive foliage, like *B. thunbergii*, which has pale green foliage that turns bright orange in autumn, and the purple-leaved *B. t.* f. *atro-purpurea*. This particular barberry is a small shrub and can be used to make a clipped hedge, the dwarf *B. t.* 'Atropurpurea Nana' can be used for a low knot-garden edging.

Generally, barberries have blue-black berries. A few have all the attractive flower and foliage features as well as colorful autumn fruit. *B. prattii* (above) is one to grow for attractive berries; they are long-lasting and daintily colored porcelain-white before turning to blush pink. *B.* × *ottawensis* 'Superba' has good purple foliage and yellow flowers, which are fol-lowed by red berries. *B. wilsoniae* makes a dense mound of blue-green foliage that takes on good autumn color accented by its coral-red berries.

Callicarpa bodinieri var. *giraldii* (above) is one of the few shrubs that can provide such a striking fuchsia-pink berry color. It is small-growing and makes a rounded deciduous shrub with bronze-tinged juve-nile foliage and clusters of pale lilac flowers along the stems in midsummer. It is best to plant several shrubs together in a small group to ensure cross-pollination and so have plenty of fruit. It is quite hardy and will grow in well-drained soil in a partly shaded spot. Look for the form *C. b.* var. *g.* 'Profusion', named for the abundance of its colorful berries.

C. japonica is a small shrub with a com-pact habit of growth; the cultivar *C. j.* 'Leucocarpa' has white fruit.

Prune the shrubs hard in spring, cutting out old wood to the ground to make way for the prolifically produced new shoots. The berry-laden branches are especially popular with flower arrangers.

Cotoneaster is probably the most popular of autumn-berry shrubs, particularly for training against walls, because its stiff branches can be espaliered, cordon-trained, and generally pruned and manipulated to any linear pattern you care to create—or they can simply be left to find their own form. Among the most widely used is the rock cotoneaster, *C. horizontalis;* its natural habit is to spread its branches like the ribs of a fish. *C. microphyllus* carries its leaves in tight clusters close to the stem, with its bright red berries studded amongst the greenery like jewels. *C.* 'Coral Beauty' (above) has glossy green leaves that show off the bright red berries. *C.* 'Cornubia' has a brilliant abundance of coral-red fruit decorating each exceedingly tall arching branch. *C.* 'Pink Champagne' has yellow berries that blush pink as they age. *C. bullatus* has particularly large oval leaves and is another tall-growing shrub, to at least 9 feet. They will grow anywhere in well-drained soil.

Euonymus planipes (below) is a curiously colored tree and a relative of the winged spindletree, *E. alatus*. It has pendent lantern-shaped berries in early autumn amid the red-tinted acid green foliage. A fuchsia-pink fleshy cup surrounds the orange berry—an outstanding combination, but this plant is not often seen in gardens. In good rich soil it will make a medium-sized tree, to about 20 feet, with a broad, spreading crown.

Gaultheria, once more commonly known as *Pernettya*, is an outstanding evergreen shrub that carries clusters of brightly colored berries, in a wide range of colors, throughout autumn. They are especially valued by florists and flower arrangers for their quite formal sprays of berries. *G. mucronata* is a small-leaved shrub with many named hybrids that positively groan under their burden of autumn fruit. But this will only happen if a male plant is located with a group of female plants, so be sure to get both sexes. They require cool, moist, acid soil and sun or partial shade.

Hybrids include *G. m.* 'Mascula' (above), *G. m.* 'Crimsonia', *G. m.* 'Mulberry Wine' with magenta berries, the lilac-pink *G. m.* 'Pink Pearl', *G. m.* 'White Pearl', and the pale pink *G. m.* 'Sea Shell'.

Hypericum androsaemum (above), a native British plant commonly known as tutsan, is one of the St. John's wort and is a small deciduous shrub that flowers from early summer through autumn. The flowers are small and bright yellow and the soft green leaves are comparatively large and oval. As with most hypericums, its stems are flushed with red. But the most striking aspect is the berries; surrounded by starlike sepals they turn from rusty red to glittering black beads. This hypericum will often continue in flower even as it goes to seed, so you get a pretty mix of yellow petals and clusters of tinted berries. It's not too fussy about the soil it's planted in or its position.

Hippophae rhamnoides (above) is commonly called sea buckthorn, since it is one of the best plants for seaside gardens. The coloring is superb in any garden, with the narrow, silvery foliage perfectly complementing the warm terracotta-orange berries that crowd the stems in autumn. Berries will be borne only if male and female shrubs are planted together to allow for cross pollination. It is a large, thorny shrub, resistant to drought, that will reach 20 feet and sucker freely, eventually making a dense thicket of sharp spiny branches.

In May, the crab apple trees in the hedgerows around my English garden burst into flower, which was always the signal to begin planning which flavor of herb jellies to make that autumn. The tart little green fruit of *Malus sylvestris* makes the most delicious base for all sorts of sweet condiments. Ornamentally those trees were not up to much, but there are many other crab apples that will decorate the autumn garden, like *M.* 'John Downie', with edible crimson-red fruit, or *M.* × *zumi* 'Golden Hornet' (right), a small spreading tree with drooping branches covered in small yellow apples. *M. hupehensis* is a good ornamental crab apple covered in a profusion of scented white flowers in spring followed by red-flushed yellow fruit in autumn.

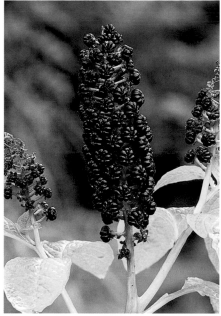

Phytolacca americana (above), or poke, is a native American perennial sometimes known as red-ink plant, since the berry juice was once used as a writing material. Long ago, the juice was also used to deepen the color of port wine—a practice long discontinued since it did nothing for the flavor, and it was later discovered that over time, the berries have a toxic effect. Poke root is an important medicinal herb, and the young shoots that emerge in late spring have been used as a potherb, although they may also have a toxic effect. In the garden it is an oddity, which is why I include it. Tall-growing, weird perennials can spice up the action, and the pokeweed's rose-madder stems and blackberry-blue berries are truly eye-catching. It needs moist soil to do well, in shade or sun.

Physalis alkekengi (above), or Chinese lantern plant, is a longtime cottage garden and flower arranger's favorite perennial. The bright papery shells surrounding the glossy orange fruit are what make it so attractive, from early summer right through autumn. During winter the shell will gradually disintegrate, leaving only the veins and exposing the fruit within a wiry skeleton cage. Its relative, *P. peruviana*, is the "designer" fruit known as cape gooseberry, the darling of gourmet chefs, who peel back the papery outer wrapping to expose the orange fruit, which is then used to decorate finished dishes. The garden perennial, which is occasionally treated as an annual, is a moderately fast colonizer and looks good in late-flowering summer borders where the sharp orange tints make a good feature. Plant it in any well-drained soil, choosing a position in partial shade to full sun. It will withstand a fair amount of neglect, which is why it is so often found in derelict gardens.

Pyracantha, or firethorn, is a fairly large group of evergreen shrubs that are often grown like cotoneaster, as climbers and wallcovering. In spring, clusters of tiny white flowers shroud the thorny branches. These are followed in autumn by clusters of berries in shades of red, orange or yellow that persist until the birds have eaten them all, if it is a lean winter, or throughout winter, if there is plenty of other food around. *P.* 'Orange Glow' (above) is the most widely used orange-berried kind, while *P. rogersiana* f. *flava* is noted for its abundant yellow berries. *P. ×* *watereri* has glossy green leaves, a compact habit, and plenty of red berries.

The plants do best in a sheltered spot in sun or part shade. To train against a wall, tie in leaders to a wire support during the first few years, then cut back the long lateral growth produced after flowering.

Rosa species and hybrids include many that produce attractive hips; probably the best known are those of *R. rugosa*. They are exceedingly round, almost bulbous, bright red and shiny. But several other roses produce curiously colored hips, and outstanding among these are the hips of *R.* 'Geranium' (right), and *R. glauca* (above). The latter is an especially good rose with faded raspberry-pink single flowers, blue-gray foliage, and pretty brick-red hips. *R.* 'Geranium' has foliage that is quite lacy in appearance and the little hips are like orange confetti scattered along the branches. *R. pimpinellifolia* makes a thicket of spiny branches covered in tiny leaves and soft pink, double flowers followed by glossy black hips. *R. nitida* has orange hips and scarlet foliage in autumn.

Species roses need room to spread out but work better in borders than hybrid teas or floribundas. Well-drained soil in a sunny spot suits best, and the only pruning needed is removing crowded stems and old, worn-out wood in early spring.

Sorbus, or mountain ash, is a widely varied genus that includes numerous small trees that have good autumn foliage, clusters of colorful fruit, or both. One such is *S. commixta* 'Embley' (right), which has fine green foliage that colors to rusty red in late autumn and heavy clusters of bright red fruit. *S. vilmorinii* (below) has pendent clusters of red fruit that fade to a pale pink or to white tinted with rose-red amid dark red autumn foliage. *S. hupehensis* is erect as a young tree, gradually spreading with age, and has fine blue-green foliage and loose panicles of faded pink berries. The one other notable characteristic is that the flower clusters often smell quite nasty; I grew *S. hupehensis* for the berries, but in early summer wondered where the smell of rotting meat was coming from—not very nice. So plant this tree well away from open windows or any areas where you sit out in the garden.

FLOWERS

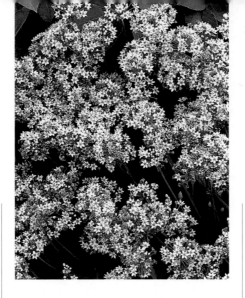

Every season has its color scheme: spring has shades of pastel blue and yellow with hints of pink; summer's palette is warmed by the passage of the days and the addition of red and orange; and then we reach autumn, when saturated colors begin to appear. Against the deepening shadows and darkening foliage, flower colors stand out all the more. Now is not the time to start putting the garden to bed for the winter, it is an occasion to celebrate the finely painted scene that nature lays out for us and from which we can draw inspiration for next year's garden glory.

Monkshoods, like *Aconitum carmichaelii* 'Arendsii' (left), is typical of the flower color found in autumn gardens. It is quite possibly the most intensely blue perennial, bearing the spikes of bell-shaped flowers on sturdy erect spikes. It does best in well-drained soil in partial shade. Weave it beneath and between autumn-coloring shrubs.

Allium tuberosum (above), with white flowers, and the purple *A. senescens* ssp. *montanum* (below), are among the late-flowering species in the popular ornamental section of the onion genus. These erect-stemmed, bulbous plants look great with grasses and do best in free-draining soil and full sun. They increase rapidly, so lift and replant the bulblets frequently. Both of these plants only reach about 18 inches, so use them near the front of borders or among groundcovering plants so that their flowers are shown off to best advantage.

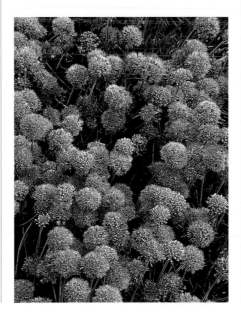

Anemone × *hybrida* 'Honorine Jobert' (below) is one of the finest autumn-flowering perennials. Anemones are sometimes called windflowers, and these in particular have a graceful movement in the soft cool breezes of the season. The erect wiry stems carry the flowers well above the

palmate foliage, and a single plant will spread steadily to make a sizable clump. As the young leaves unfurl in late summer they have a silky, filamented surface, so the plant looks good for most of its time in the garden. They do best in moisture-retentive soil in full sun or partial shade. *A.* × *h.* 'Max Vogel' has rosy pink, semidouble flowers, and *A. hupehensis* var. *japonica* 'Prinz Heinrich' has single pink ones. Mix them up for an informal planting among pink and white autumn-berried shrubs.

Aster, the Michaelmas daisy, is probably the ultimate autumn perennial flower. At this time of year, few other plants can compete with the range of color, height, and flower size found in this genus, as can be plainly seen in the nursery rows at Waterperry gardens (above) in Oxfordshire, England. Dan Hinkley, proprietor of Heronswood Nursery in Washington state, has written most eloquently about the true value of asters, "When the leaves have crisped on the Golden Hops, the grasses have splayed and even the fruiting plants have lost their luster, it is the asters that bring clarity to the season and reason to continue with garden strolls in the evening." The various named cultivars are taken from two species; *A. novae-angliae* and *A. novi-belgii*. The first are much more vigorous and disease resistant, while the second are prone to mildew attacks that corrupt the foliage and weaken the plant and so must be regularly sprayed. Then there are the species that offer the gardener a limited range of color but a huge selection of height, from the ground-hugging 6-inch-tall *A. dumosus* to the towering *A. umbellatus* at nearly 6 feet. Generally hardy plants, they require little attention and prefer well-drained, good soil in sun or partial shade. The plants benefit from mulching to keep the roots moist in dry spells.

A. cordifolius 'Aldebaran' (left) makes a loose open plant with clusters of lilac-white flowers. *A. divaricatus* (above) has tiny starlike flowers on open wiry branches. *A. × frikartii* 'Mönch' (above) makes sturdy clumps about 18 inches tall. *A. novi-belgii* 'Saint Egwyn' (below) is pink flowered, and *A. amellus* 'Veilchenkönigin' (right) is typical of the rich coloring found among Michaelmas daisies. This type makes healthy, clump-forming plants about 12 to 18 inches tall.

Bupleurum fruticosum (above) is an ever-green perennial that makes quite a sizable mound of blue-green foliage topped by umbells of brassy yellow flowers. It does well in gardens near the sea, and likes a well-drained soil in full sun. A much finer plant is *B. falcatum* which grows to only about 1 foot tall and has lacy umbels of tiny yellow flowers. It has a pleasant habit of self-seeding itself through grasses and among annual flowers.

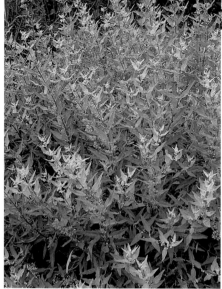

Caryopteris × *clandonensis* 'Arthur Simmonds' (above) is a small deciduous shrub that is invaluable for the fine blue flowers it carries along the length of its wandlike branches. It does best if cut back hard each spring to promote new shoots, and it likes well-drained soil in full sun. The leaves of *C.* × *c.* 'Worcester Gold' (left) have a pale yellow cast that perfectly sets off the light blue of the flowers.

Choisya ternata (above), the Mexican orange, is a glossy leafed, evergreen shrub that carries highly fragrant white flowers in late summer through autumn. The flowering tips of the branches can be damaged by frost, but just cut away the scorched leaves and it will soon have new shoots. It does well in any well-drained but moisture-retentive soil, in sun or partial shade.

Chrysanthemum 'Belle', with red flowers, yellow-flowered *C.* 'Honey' (left), and brick-red *C.* 'Louise' (above) are good examples of the late-flowering border chrysanthemums. Along with Michaelmas daisies, these are among the showiest of autumn-flowering perennials and will flower dependably even if totally neglected, as I know, having been a very lax chrysanthemum grower! They are excellent cut flowers and easy to care for in the garden, requiring well-drained soil and full sun.

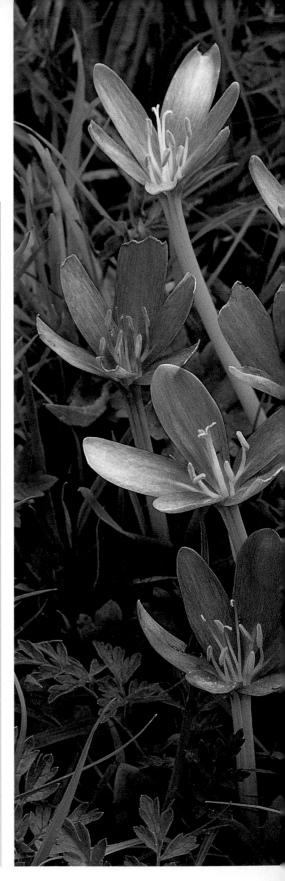

Cleome hasslerana (above) is commonly called spider flower. It is a showy half-hardy annual that quickly grows from an early-spring sowing, (done when all chance of frost is past) to eventually reach at least 4 feet in height. The flowers are scented and top each stiffly erect stem with blooms in shades of pink, white, and mauve. It makes a good show in mixed borders and among shrubs, and likes well-drained but moisture-retentive soil in sun or partial shade.

Clerodendrum bungei (above) is a tall-growing shrub (to at least 8 feet) that has broad, dark green leaves and umbels of flowers that are red in bud and fade to lilac-pink—quite a vivid show. The stems are dark and stiffly erect, and the shrub suckers quite freely, so it will in time form a dense thicket. Frost can cut it down, but it will soon shoot again. Watch out for the leaves, which smell bad when crushed. Plant in any soil, in sun or partial shade.

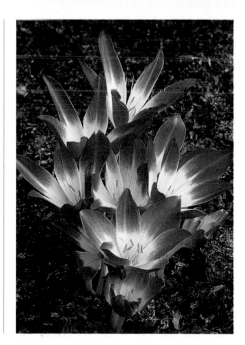

Colchicum autumnale (left), *C. speciosum* (above), and *C. bivonae* (right) are all hardy autumn-flowering plants that grow from corms planted in the spring. The flowers are sometimes called naked ladies because the leaves do not appear until after the flowers have faded, making large clumps of broad, straplike, bright green foliage that endure for most of the winter and well into spring. Several flowers appear from each corm.

Colchicums do best planted in an open sunny position and well-drained soil. They work well among deciduous shrubs or naturalized in tall grass that is only cut during late summer.

Crinum × *powellii* (above) is a tall-growing bulbous perennial that has drooping trumpet-shaped flowers atop thick stems. The flowers are scented and, like colchicums, appear before the foliage. Crinums are not completely hardy, so plant in a sunny, sheltered spot in deeply dug, rich soil that is well-drained but does not dry out.

Crocosmia 'Star of the East' (above) is a clump-forming perennial with superior late-summer to early-autumn flowers. This variety has glowing bright orange flowers, but there are other species and cultivars that take on colors from yellow (*C.* × *c.* 'Golden Fleece') to deep crimson (*C.* 'Lucifer'). *C.* 'Emily Mackenzie' is popular for its wide-open flowers, where most other crocosmias have rather closed tubular blossoms. *C.* 'Solfatare' has warm apricot-colored flowers and the foliage is flushed with warm brown; it looks quite striking when grown with *Stipa arundinacea*. These plants grow from corms and gradually increase to form sizable clumps. They like full sun and well-drained soil.

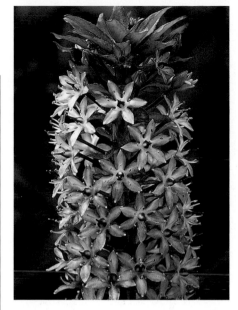

Cyclamen hederifolium (above) is a hardy cyclamen that grows wild in the woods and meadows of the sunny Mediterranean countries. It grows from corms and can be easily increased from seed sown fresh in late autumn or as soon as it ripens. As the flowers fade, the stem curls up, drawing the seed capsule down to corm level. When the capsule ripens, the coil springs out, shooting the seed all around. The trick is to catch the pod just before this happens and release the sticky little seeds into some good sandy compost. Plant corms just below the soil surface in full sun or partial shade, in well-drained soil.

Dahlia is a genus that offers a huge array of highly colorful flowers in all sorts of shapes and sizes, from tight little pompons to great spidery objects like *D.* 'Reputation' (above), and they are divided into groups according to the type of flower they have: single, waterlily, collarette, cactus, and so on. Dahlias are tender perennials that grow from tubers, which are generally lifted after flowering and overwintered with protection from frost; a dusting with fungicide protects the resting tubers from botrytis. In spring, the tubers begin to shoot and plants can then be increased by removing the shoots and rooting them in trays of compost. Dahlias require a good well-dug soil that is well drained but does not dry out. Plant them in a sunny spot. Tall-growing varieties will need staking.

Eucomis bicolor (above), the pineapple flower, is an exotic-looking bulbous plant that is hardy if given a thick blanket of mulch in winter. I have grown these in containers and enjoyed as much as the starry little flowers the fleshy seedpods that array themselves along the flower spike. In fact, *Eucomis* seeded itself into the paving cracks beneath the pots, so it must be quite robust. Put three or four bulbs into large urns or tubs for best effect. They like full sun and well-drained soil.

Euphorbia seguieriana (above) is a showy perennial about 18 inches tall, with acid green terminal flower clusters in spring that turn to bright green buttons atop autumn-colored stems. Another euphorbia that gives good autumn value is the clump-forming *E. nicaeensis*; the foliage is a cool blue-gray, the flowers and pods more yellow than green, and the stems turn bright red in autumn. Dark red tinged with green is the predominant year-round color of *E. dulcis* 'Chameleon'; it seeds freely and spreads by underground stems. These plants prefer well-drained soil in full sun.

Fuchsia flowers are one of autumn's great delights; there are all sorts of combinations of the red, pink, purple, and white coloring and all sizes of flower—from frou-frou doubles as full as a ballerina's skirts to skeletal singles with needle-narrow petals, and all with a graceful pendent habit. Combine this with bright foliage, as in *F. magellanica* 'Versicolor' (above), and the plant becomes a double-feature winner in the autumn garden. Fuchsias do well in full sun or part shade and well-drained soil that does not dry out.

Gentiana 'Strathmore' (above) is one of the finest blue-flowered plants in the garden, no matter what the season. The huge blue trumpets nestle neatly into the narrow, dark green, glossy foliage in a most comfortable manner, making a vibrant carpet in a rock garden or raised bed. Gentians need neutral to acid soils that are rich in humus or well-rotted compost and never dry out. *G. sino-ornata* is another autumn-flowering gentian that carries white-throated, azure-blue flowers atop rosettes of grassy foliage. It does especially well in acid soil near a water feature, since it likes a moist atmosphere.

Helenium 'Bruno' (above) is one of several sneezeweed cultivars that contribute sturdy daisylike flowers to the autumn border. This is a bushy perennial about 2 to 3 feet in height, with sprays of dusky red flowers in late summer through autumn. It does best in well-drained soil in full sun.

Hedera helix (above), or common ivy, might not seem like a first choice for inclusion among colorful autumn flowers, but the balls of bright green blooms against the glossy malachite of the evergreen foliage are really quite striking. These eventually turn to little black berries and constitute a feature that often goes unnoticed. It pays to be aware of all the attributes a plant possesses, not just the most obvious ones; you never know what you will discover and be able to use to good effect in a plant grouping.

Helianthus × *multiflorus* 'Capenoch Star' (below) is a perennial relative of the annual sunflower, *H. annuus*, and makes a branching, tall-growing plant to about 4 feet tall, with lemon-yellow flowers at the end of each stem. The perennial sunflowers can be invasive, so allow plenty of space, although regular lifting and dividing will go some way towards keeping them in check. The willow-leafed sunflower, *H. salicifolius*, is particularly invasive. But for a colorful autumn screen of bright sunny flowers it is hard to beat, since it reaches nearly 7 feet tall when growing in the right conditions of sun and well-drained soil.

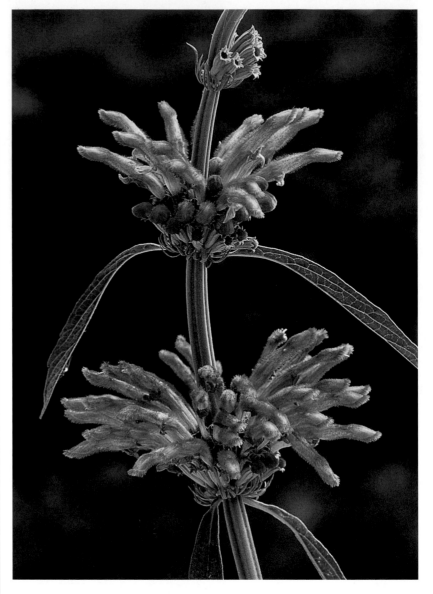

Impatiens tinctoria (above) is a native of the moist mountain forests of northern Africa, so it is only perennial in mild climates and with protection. The flowers are large and orchidlike, and the broad oval leaves are dark green. It will do well in deep, rich, moist soil and looks especially pretty naturalized among trees or tall-growing shrubs. The other *Impatiens* that is fun to grow is the white-flowered form of the Peruvian balsam, *I. glandulifera* 'Candida'—as long as you do not let it get out of hand. It seeds freely, so take care, but the tall, up to 6 feet, stems of pure white flowers really are eye-catching if left to colonize at the edge of woodland.

Leonotis leonurus (above), or lion's-ear, is a semievergreen shrub, up to 4 feet tall, with loose open branches and whorls of bright orange, slightly felted flowers. It is not fully hardy, so it does best with a sunny, sheltered position in well-drained soil— moisture around the base of the plant will cause it to rot. It looks nifty mixed up with the tall stems and purple flowers of *Verbena bonariensis*.

Leycesteria formosa (right), or Himalayan honeysuckle, has its place in the autumn garden because of its curiously laid-back pendent blooms—dark purple bracts tipped by tiny white true flowers. It should be cut to the ground in spring. It will quickly send up new stems that are up to 5 feet tall. It does well in sun or part shade and well-drained soil, and makes a good quick screening plant.

Liriope muscari (above), or lily turf, is a groundcovering evergreen, making spreading clumps of long, narrow, dark green leaves, from which emerge spikes of lavender-purple flowers in late summer. The plants spread by underground rhizomes and do well in dry freely draining soil in sun or partial shade. Only about 1 foot in height and spreading to about 18 inches, *Liriope* can also be used as an edging. There are varieties with variegated leaves like *L. m.* 'Gold-banded' and *L. m.* 'Variegata', but their foliage will scorch in hot sun.

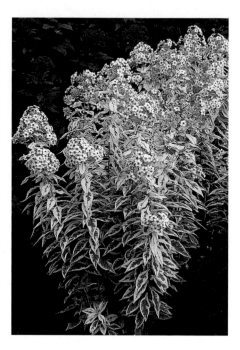

Persicaria amplexicaulis (below) spreads quickly to make a dense, clumping thicket of lax stems that carry pokers of bright pink flowers in autumn. I like to see it among the hip-bearing branches of species roses like *Rosa glauca*. The cultivar *P. a.* 'Firetail' has more reddish tinted flowers than the species. Commonly called knotweed, it can be invasive, but is easily pulled out from where it is not wanted. It does best in moisture-retentive soil, in sun or part shade. *P. affinis* is a mat-forming dwarf relative that makes tiny, intensely pink spikes in autumn; it looks great tumbling down a wall. *P. affinis* 'Darjeeling Red' is especially well colored.

Nerine bowdenii (above) is an autumn-flowering bulb that makes a spectacular show when planted in bold masses. Each flower head is composed of about eight to ten individual blooms in bright fuchsia-pink. These top stiffly erect stems that are roughly 18 inches tall. Like colchicums and crinums, the flowers of nerines appear before the foliage. When planting the bulbs, put them in open sandy soil in a sunny spot with their "noses" just below the soil surface; they do best if they bake during summer. Once established, the colony should be left alone since they do not take kindly to being disturbed. Feed occasionally with a potash-rich plant food.

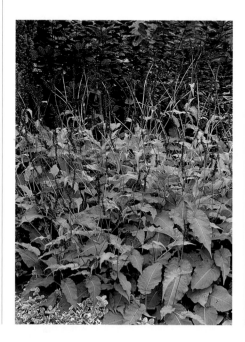

Phlox paniculata 'Norah Leigh' (above) is remarkable among the autumn-flowering cottage garden favorites for its cream varie-gated foliage. In fact, I feel the flowers get lost among the bright foliage, but the total effect creates a brilliant spot in the garden. Phlox do best in well-drained soil in sun and slowly increase to make sizable clumps of sweetly scented flowers. Other phlox have plain green foliage but brilliant flower color: *P. p.* 'Amethyst', with violet-blue flowers; *P. p.* 'Bright Eyes', which has white flowers dotted pink in the center; *P. p.* 'Fujiyama', pure white and prolific, and *P. p.* 'Blue Ice', which is almost, but not quite blue.

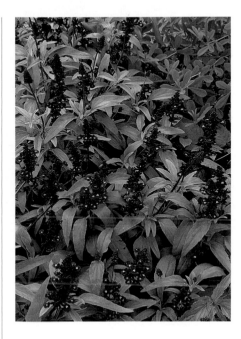

Rudbeckia fulgida is an American prairie perennial, a robust plant that makes a pool of golden sunshine wherever it grows. In England, I grew the variety *R. f.* var. *deamii*, (above right) with *Stipa arundinacea*, because the orange autumn tint of the grass looked so good with the rudbeckia and reminded me, in a sideways manner, of the prairies of my home state, Illinois. Rudbeckias are also half-hardy annuals. The most outrageous is probably *hirta* 'Kelvedon Star', with the base of each petal heavily blotched with chocolate brown. Another equally strange perennial is *R. occidentalis* 'Green Wizard', which has big, black central cones surrounded by bright green sepals—there are no petals on this aberration. *R.* 'Indian Summer' (above left) is a good simple flower with bright petals and a small central boss. Plant in well-drained soil in sun.

Salvia farinacea (above), or mealycup sage, is a perennial sage that is usually grown as a half-hardy annual bedding plant. It is roughly 1 foot tall, and the rich purple-blue color looks good with grasses and other late-summer and early-autumn plants. *S. f.* 'Strata' is a fine baby-blue cultivar. The seeds should be sown in spring and then pricked out to make plants for setting out in early summer. Other annual salvias are *S. splendens*, with *S. s.* 'Red Arrows' being especially vibrant, and *S. coccinea* 'Cherry Blossom', which is a pretty bicolor of pink and white. Plant in full sun in well-drained soil.

Perennial sages, apart from the ever-popular culinary herb, *S. officinalis*, are

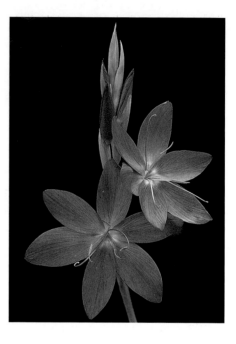

Schizostylis coccinea 'Sunrise' (above), commonly known as crimson flat or Kaffir lily, is a rhizomatous perennial that does best in full sun and well-drained soil that has had plenty of rotted compost added. It makes a terrific cut flower, so set out a row in the kitchen garden for indoor flower arrangements. It is one of those spiky plants that look good with cascading grasses or popping up from clumps of mounding or groundcovering herbs, such as *Salvia officinalis* 'Tricolor' with its purple and pink markings. *Schizostylis coccinea* 'Mrs. Hegarty' is bright pink and vigorous and *S. c.* 'Viscountess Byng' has dependable autumn flowers in soft pink. *S. c.* 'Major' has large pink flowers.

also wonderfully decorative, and among the prettiest is the frost-tender Mexican sage bush, *S. leucantha* (above). It has heavily veined leaves that are silvery and felted on the reverse but dark green above. The flower spikes also have some of the fuzziness of the foliage. It makes an open branching shrub reaching a height of about 2 feet.

As a complete contrast, *S. verticillata* 'Purple Rain' (above center) has finely cut leaves that give the whole plant an open lacy texture, above which the dark purple flower spikes float happily. Neither of these plants seems particularly hardy, so it is advisable to take cuttings each summer to propagate for next year's planting. One other salvia worth growing for its showiness is *S. sclarea* var. *turkestanica*, which is biennial and self-seeds freely. It makes a tall, open branching plant with huge fuzzy leaves and large, pale purple and white flower bracts. It is rather smelly (one common name is housemaid's armpit).

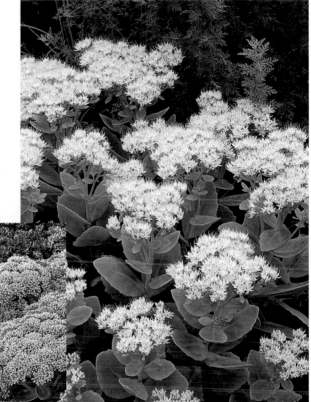

Sedum is unquestionably the autumn stalwart genus, although these plants look good most of the year. They are hardy perennials that make clumps of fleshy stems with soft fleshy leaves and have flower umbels variously tinted white to rosy pink. One of the very best is the small-growing *S.* 'Bertram Anderson' (above), a small-leafed sort that makes a spreading clump of silvery green leaves that are tinted purplish pink and topped with a mass of rosy red flowers in late summer to early autumn.

S. middendorffianum var. *diffusum* (center right) is unique for the multicolored flower heads each plant carries. It has the fleshy foliage characteristic of the genus, but the flowers are its strong point. *S. spectabile* 'Iceberg' (far right) is one of the palest flowered, being a good clean white above fine green foliage. Both of these make medium-size plants.

Some sedums, like *S. telephium* 'Matrona' and *S. t.* 'Munstead Red' that have a deep red cast to the leaves. I think these are the best types, but I am partial to red and brown plants anyway: They make a solid mass against which lighter textured plants can be played to good effect. Their succulence means that sedums withstand drought very well and they enjoy a place in full sun. Soil that is too rich makes them flaccid, so "lean and mean" gets the best results.

Solidago rugosa 'Fireworks' (above) is one of the prettiest goldenrods, sending out sprays of soft yellow blooms on arching stems about 18 to 24 inches long. It is remarkably delicate when compared to its coarser sisters—a floral Cinderella. Goldenrods do make good garden plants —the ragged conical heads of sharp yellow make a good backdrop to stronger flower shapes and more demanding colors.

Solidago tends to spread like wildfire, so make sure you have the room and the will to control it. It grows just about anywhere, but full sun and free-draining soil are preferred.

Tricyrtis hirta (above), the toad lily, is a bit of a curiosity, and not one that I am wild about, although it is a good autumn-flowering plant. Perhaps it doesn't have enough substance to suit my taste for showiness at this time of year. The spotted starry flowers sit atop rigid stems that emerge from ground-hugging, spotted foliage. It probably looks best among ferns in a midsummer-night's-dream setting of moist, warm soil in part shade.

Verbena bonariensis (above) has been one of my favorite plants ever since I saw it growing in naturalized masses in the remains of a Gertrude Jekyll garden, back in 1981. The area was a derelict iris garden on either side of a sunken path—the intention being that the iris blooms would be viewed at eye level. The verbena, with its whippy stems and glorious lavender-purple flowers, had just about taken over, so all one could do was look down the throats of the tiny little trumpets, noting the orange speck at the base—knockout! I've been devoted ever since. A remnant of that memory exists in an iris bed I once planted, scattering this verbena among the rhizomes so that after the irises faded, there was something to look at other than the gray-green iris leaves. It will seed just about anywhere.

Zephyranthes candida (above) is the ever-green rain lily, of which I am becoming increasingly aware, since it has naturalized in my front lawn in Texas. John Fairey, of the famous Peckerwood Garden Foundation near Houston, has been responsible for introducing a large selection of these plants from Mexico. There is a yellow-flowered species, *Z. citrina,* a purple tinted one, *Z. atamasco,* and *Z. grandiflora,* which is charmingly pink. In late summer and early autumn, the rain brings them into bloom after the dry dormant period of summer. They naturalize quickly in rich, well-drained soil, and the ripe seed heads can be shaken like maracas to scatter the seed, which will surely germinate. They are really only half-hardy, although they will succeed in cool-climate gardens if given a sheltered spot.

Zinnia, like *Dahlia,* provides a wide range of flower color and size, and no autumn garden would be complete without a contribution from this genus. Native to the warm southwestern United States and Mexico, zinnias are half-hardy annuals and should be sown in the early spring to plant out after all hint of frost has left the garden. Shown here is *Z. haageana* 'Chippendale' (above), and it is typical of the loose, cheerful, branching clumps that this annual will form. Deadhead regularly to keep in flower, and plant in a well-drained soil in full sun for the very best flowers.

PHOTO ACKNOWLEDGMENTS

I am very grateful to the following garden owners and designers for allowing me to take pictures and for providing invaluable assistance and support (L=left; C=center; R=right; T=top; B=bottom): Abbey Dore Garden, Herefordshire, Charis Ward 22–23, 26, 32–33, 43, 71, 126L, 142, 144C, 146, 147R; Bath Botanic Gardens, Somerset 12–13, 18–19, 38, 133T; Batsford Arboretum, Gloucestershire 14, 118R; Le Berquerie, Varengeville-sur-Mer, Normandy, France, Mark Brown 62, 64, 84R, 134C, 149LB, 158L; Beth Chatto Gardens, Essex, Beth Chatto 50, 52, 68, 132R, 134R, 135T, 140C/front cover, 141R, 143R, 150RB, 150RT, 156L; Bois des Moutiers, Varengeville-sur-Mer, Normandy, France, Mme. Mary Mallet 65, 108–109, 124L; Castelnau, Barnes, London, Gay Search, designer Dan Pearson 2–3, 135B; Chiltern Road, Wendover, Bucks, Jo Chatterton 144L; Clos Normand, Varengeville-sur-Mer, Normandy, France, Mme. Constance Kargére 80, 124C; Cotswold Garden Flowers, Worcestershire, Bob Brown 21, 56, 138; The Dingle, Welshpool, Powys, Roy and Barbara Joseph 4, 15, 24, 25, 111, 116–117, 120L, 121R, 121L, 122L, 122R, 125R, 126–127, 128B, 134L, 140L, 145B; Dinmore Manor, Herefordshire, R. G. Murray 18L; Dolwen, Llanrhaeadr, Powys, Frances Denby 5/139R/back cover, 34; The Old Vicarage, East Ruston, Norfolk, Alan Gray and Graham Robeson 7, 36–37, 100–101, 101, 106, 112, 114, 115, 124–125, 129R, 141L; Eastgrove Cottage Garden, Worcestershire, Malcolm and Carol Skinner 95, 127C, 151L, 162L; Elsing Hall, Norfolk, Shirley and David Cargill 130L; Great Dixter, East Sussex, Christopher Lloyd 1/155C, 41, 46, 66–67, 70, 81, 84L, 93, 102–103, 120C, 137, 147CB, 147CT, 150L, 152C,

152–153, 153T, 155R, 157RB, 157L, 160L, 161LB, 161R, 164–165, 164L, 165R; Green Farm Plants, Hampshire, J. Coke 45, 57, 97; Hergest Croft, Herefordshire, W. L and R. A. Banks 8, 118L; The Hiller Garden, Worcestershire, designer Bob Brown 9, 58, 59, 63, 79, 110, 144R, 149LT, 154R, 160R, 161LT, 162R, 163L; Holker Hall, Cumbria, Lord and Lady Cavendish 19R, 122C, 128T; Leila Cabot Perry Garden, Museum of American Impressionism, Giverny, France, designer Mark Brown 60–61; The Lodge, Sussex, Mr. and Mrs. Upton 90–91; Merriments, East Sussex, Mark Buchele 76–77, 145T; Picton Garden, Herefordshire, Paul Picton 156R, 143L; Powis Castle, Powys, National Trust 6–7, 130R; RHS Gardens, Wisley 55, 117, 131, 136, 148LB, 151CB, 151RT, 153B, 157C, 163C; Stockton Bury, Herefordshire, Raymond Treasure and Gordon Fenn 30, 121C; Sycamore Barn, Norfolk, Ethne Clarke 96; Upper Mill Cottage, Kent, David and Mavis Seeney 10–11, 13, 51, 87, 89, 107, 132CB, 133B, 155L, 155C, 158R, 164C; Valley Gardens (Windsor Great Park), Surrey 119, 120R, 123T, 123B, 125C, 140R; Waterperry Gardens, Oxfordshire 39, 44–45, 82, 83, 98, 129L, 129C, 139L, 148LT, 149R; West Dean Gardens, West Sussex 47, 72–73, 73, 74, 75, 94, 132CT, 159L, 165C; White Windows, Hampshire, Jane Sterndale-Bennett 31, 42, 127R, 148R, 152L, 156C, 159R, 160C, 162C, 163R.

In addition to the above I would like to thank Fergus Garrett, Mark Flanagan, Ruth and Sam Buckley, Jim Buckland, and Sarah Wain for their help with this project, and Ethne Clarke for her faith in it.

Jonathan Buckley

BIBLIOGRAPHY

Chatto, Beth. *Beth Chatto's Green Tapestry*. Trafalgar Square, 1999.

Clarke, Ethne, and Clive Nichols. *Herb Garden Design*. Macmillan, 1995.

Clarke, Ethne. *Gardening with Foliage Plants: Leaf, Bark, and Berry*. Abbeville Press, Inc., 1997.

Fish, Margery. *A Flower for Every Day*. London: The Garden Book Club, 1965.

Hayward, Gordon.

Garden Paths: A New Way to Solve Practical Problems in the Garden. Houghton Mifflin, 1998.

Garden Paths: Inspiring Designs and Practical Projects. Firefly Books, 1997.

Jekyll, Gertrude. *Colour Schemes for the Flower Garden*. Antique Collector's Club, 1994.

Larkcom, Joy. *Creative Vegetable Gardening*. Abbeville Press, Inc., 1997.

Ogden, Scott. *Gardening Success with Difficult Soils*. Taylor, 1992.

Phillips, Roger and Martyn Rix.

The Random House Book of Shrubs. Random House, 1989.

The Random House Book of Perennials. Vols. 1 & 2. Random House, 1992.

Robinson, William.

The English Flower Garden. Sagapress, 1995.

The Wild Garden. Sagapress, 1994.

Waters, Alice. *Chez Panisse Vegetables*. HarperCollins Publishers, Inc., 1996.

Wilder, Louise Beebe. *Adventures with Hardy Bulbs*. The Lyons Press, 1998.

INDEX